My Jeep Grille Adventures: Camp Kitchen & Cookbook
Author: Mark M. DeNittis
Photos by: Mark M. DeNittis
www.JeepGrilleAdventures.com ©2007
A division of Rocky Mountain Trade Enterprise, LLC
www.RockyMountainTrade.com

Forward: "Road Trip"

Excerpt from my life journal Jeep Log Date: sometime in 1999:

Life on the road twists and turns. Leaving southern sunny beaches for Rocky Mountain High, high you say, has one ever been low on the road?! So many miles, countless hours paved and unpaved. Where in life? What point in life? The past left at the Devil's Golf Course. All was shunned, the lights of the City of Sin were dimmed. The sands of the dunes shifted like soft sand of a Cape Cod beach through a child's fingers. One would have never thought standing tall like the saguaro cactus of Arizona. From lowland desert to ponderosa pine to red rock canyons, the terrain changes as quickly as life. Where in life? What point...the beginning?

Atop the mountain looking back, at what...nothing. At the ridge... the ridge of day and night where time ceases to exist and the moment transpires. Five hundred miles gone, five years done!

Life on the road never ending, each turn is like the dawn above the Chihos Mountains of South Texas where the true sound of silence can be heard. How does one hear the sound of silence? Go...Go...Go...open your eyes, your mind and absorb, as the desert floor absorbs the suns warmth. See the time stand still...hear the sound of silence. Open your eyes... open your mind.

Moon over the mountains, the crisp air carries the coyote's cry. In the distance hear the language...hear the elders speak. The light of the moon embraces, let it caress your soul. The coyote speaks... yearning for time of now.

Tell me now...sit still my love...still, hear the sound of silence...see the time stand still. Let the light of the moon embrace and caress. Come on this journey, see as I have seen, hear as I have heard, feel as I have felt.

Atop the canyon, looking southward, the pines stand tall, as does the canyon above the river. The river flows swiftly as does the mind, never stopping unless parched by the sun.

The warm spring air...canyon and pine breathe it in as if it were your last. Intoxicated with the aroma... breathe as I have breathed, hear as I have heard, see as I have seen, feel as I have felt.

Valley of the God's, majestic as is ours. Standing…looking…overseeing, watching this barren land. Guiding those that travel and traveling with those that guide.

What lies ahead? Take my hand in this journey. Follow me… lead me…walk with me!

It has been in the blink of an eye that brings me here, as will in the blink of an eye take us there.

Our first camp trip as a family Viv was 2.

Dedication

This book is dedicated to my wife January, that supports me even though I have spent a small fortune on the "Heep" as she lovingly refers. To my daughter Vivianna for the inspiration of watching life unfold from a new perspective. Our newborn son Matteo for the joys of watching life unfold yet once again. Of course 4-Lo-Rose for being a patient and trustworthy co-pilot of multiple off-road adventures.

Acknowledgements

A very special thanks to my wife January, daughter Vivianna, son Matteo and trail-bound Jeep-hound 4-Lo Rose. Thanks to my mom and dad for raising me in nothing but the best off-road vehicles and instilling in me the love of travel and adventure. My Grandma D for all the inspirational words of wisdom and spinach and eggs with the bread made from the pool of flour. To Grammy and Grampy for taking care of me as I grew and always feeding me so well. My aunt Rita for being there when needed and trying to keep me on the straight and narrow. The Matos family for allowing me to get on my feet and giving me the opportunity to get ahead. Thanks J.M. for kicking my ass and challenging me to grow both professionally and personally. My good friends Brian "The Iceman", Joe (SPF2), 'da boys: Jay, Paul, Mikey and many others from good ole "Worm Town".

All the good folks back in Elkins, West Virginia, Jill and Mom. I haven't forgotten that I still owe you dinner for helping out when we buried my Bronco up on Rich Mountain. To the memory of Mike at the Church Key Pub and the jug 'o shine behind the counter, thanks Mike may you rest in peace!

To my local Denver 4x4 bud's Josh and Darren of www.CraneHiClearance.com & www.Crawlertech4x4.com and Mitch Hess of RMHE Enterprises inclusive of all the members of the "Saturday Country Club" that have aided in my insightful and gained expertise of the pedal, wheel, trail and wrench.

A big thanks to the entire gang at www.4X4Wire.com allowing me to create "Trail Bites" article series and grow into the amateur writer I am, even if I never did figure out the HTML thing.

To PhD McGrail, one of my former English teachers, (actually my worst subject in H.S.) "stop masticating on that glutinous material" may you rest in peace!

Finally to the many other wonderful and not so wonderful folks, way too numerous to name I have met along this road called life.

A super, special big humongous thanks to my editing company:

M.O.M. Inc.

Table of Contents

2000 when I first started the JGA concept, Vivianna (below left) was barely one…

…and finally, in 2007, seven years after starting, Vivianna's brother (above right) Matteo at age 5-months, helps put the finishing touches on the JGA concept. July 30th, 2007

"Thanks for the inspiration my little, Coocha-looch and Matoocha-looch!

Conosca questi i miei bambini…tutto nella questa vita è per amore della famiglia, paese e patria! Naturalmente molti ringraziamenti al Dio!

Introduction

 <u>My Jeep Grille Adventures</u> is a collection of fond memories of family, friends, food, and special places. An inspirational book for those with a love and desire for adventure, travel, the outdoors and responsible off-roading, this book focuses mostly on my experiences with foods and trails of the Rocky Mountain region and southwest.

 Since I can recall there has been an element of the outdoors and food creativity in my life. Memories of dad taking me on hunting trips to Patten, Maine eating wonderful fresh Venison Burgers with Swiss cheese and French dressing. All the wonderful garden vegetables, from both my parents and grandparents gardens. My Grampy drying eggplant and zucchini from the second floor clothesline, canning, and making piccalilli. All the sardines and crackers, pig's feet, Cape Cod conch salad, conch fritters, and flavorful dandelion and tomato wines. Grammy Emma's meatballs, braciola and cavatelli, roasted sheep head, pig's ears and feet, and those unforgettable Friday night open-face grilled cheese and mustard sandwiches. Grandma D's mustard greens with eggs and bread and Grandpa D's concord wine that bit 'ya in the boo-boo if you weren't careful. The summers spent with my cousins on Cape Cod, on the Bass River with Auntie Shirley's Zuppa de Pesche, and who could forget the periwinkles, eaten one by one, each delicately picked with a safety pin. Uncle Mike's Christmas clams casino and marinated octopus. All the fresh seafood caught off of Race Point; bluefish, striped bass, squid, clams and lobsters cooked ever so wonderfully by the tailgate of, "Mellow Yellow", my trusty old Chevy K-5 Blazer, and the '85 and '88 Ford Broncos. Auntie Rita's special pan seared grilled cheeses and chicken cacciatore. All the many family gatherings over the years that left you immobile due to the massive amounts of food consumed.

 Of course one can't forget the college years with things like American Style Burrito cooked via clothes iron or Fourth of July beer-can eggs on the campfire, that crazy late night garlic omelet recipe (not quite what we expected), crawfish boils with grilled perch, and Largemouth Bass in Foil out at the cabin in Rutland. The stew of, baby bluefish, oranges, and jug wine on the dunes of Race Point, or the freshly caught grilled fish on the beach hibachi in Key West.

Since leaving home in 1993 my travels have not just brought me life experiences. Nor as one person once told me; "you're just on one big long term vacation!!"! For me the perpetual vacation has been and continues to be an exciting opportunity to see a broad range of cuisines and cultures which are so intricately intertwined, offering the opportunity for some adventures and misadventures such as, Rich Mountain, the southern West-by-God-Virginia spirits didn't like us Yankees wheeling around up there.

One of the many reasons for <u>My Jeep Grille Adventures Cookbook</u> was to paint a picture of an American landscape not visited by most. Since first moving to Colorado in 1995 I've traded in the full size wheeling machines of my youth. In September of 1996 I bought a brand new 1997 Jeep Wrangler TJ. I can actually be quoted as once saying "I won't wheel, modify or tear this thing up like I have previous vehicles, it will be a street queen"….. YEAH RIGHT!!!

The following are recollections, reflections and recipes of backcountry trails, and small towns often not seen by the masses but viewed from the windshield of my Jeep. So sit back, put your life gears into Four-Lo, Creeper Gear, Granny Gear or whatever you will… and enjoy <u>My Jeep Grille Adventures: Camp Kitchen and Cookbook</u>.

Remember: "The World is your Oyster…put some Hot Sauce on it and chug it down"!!

Street Queen THIS! Poison Spider Waterfall 2006

Trail Preparations:

Basic Kitchen Needs, Mother Nature's Kitchen, Safety, Sanitation and Being Environmentally Aware, Go Green!

First things first, what will I need to cook out on the trail and where does all this stuff fit in an already overloaded vehicle? The following is a simple guide of tools you may need for successful outdoor cookery. Realize that a one-day trip could turn into an overnight stay by getting stuck or having a vehicular breakdown, thus over-preparedness is not a bad thing. Extra water or fluids and high-energy snacks may be a lifesaver.

Simple one-day outings:

- Cooking Thermometer (The tire gauge of the culinary world)
- Cooler & Freezer Ice Packs
- Various Snacks
- 1-gallon water per person and 1/2 gallon per animal (especially in desert or high altitude areas).
- Ingredients or pre-made recipe for your favorite lunch or dinner on the trail.
- Trash Bags to Pack out trash

Outings lasting overnight:

- Cooking Thermometer (The tire gauge of the culinary world)
- Cooler & Freezer Ice Packs
- 1-gallon of water per person and ½ gallon per animal per day.
- Various Snacks and Munchies
- Dinner, Breakfast and Lunch
- Lighter/Matches
- Cooking equipment; Fuel, stove, pots, pan, plates, utensils
- Trash Bags to pack out trash

Outings lasting 3 or more days:

- Cooking Thermometer (The tire gauge of the culinary world)
- Heavy duty Cooler with freezer packs, or 12-volt battery powered cooler.
- 1-gallon of water per person and ½ gallon per animal per day.
- Various Snacks and Munchies

- Dinner, Breakfast and Lunch
- Lighter/Matches
- Cooking equipment; Fuel, stove, pots, pan, plates, utensils
- Trash Bags HEAVY DUTY to pack out trash

Important information regarding food safety:

Cold Food Storage: Any standard 48-quart cooler will work well packed with frozen ice packs. Don't go for the cheap ones look for thermally insulated units that have temperature/days specifications. There are some 12-volt battery powered models available in sporting good sections of most major stores now that are moderately priced. The ARB cooler/freezer combination and others like it; are great investments if you have the finances. The units can be above the $500.00 range. This unit is tried, tested and proven on the roughest terrain and safaris into the Outback of Australia and Wilds of Africa.

Dry Ice dangers: Although dry ice will easily keep foods super cold, it could just as easily give you freezer burn if touched with bare skin. I do not recommend this, especially when young children are along for the trip.

Frozen Foods: Freezing pre-made foods in advance for simple heating on the trail has a dual purpose; to keep foods cold and safe and they double as an additional freezer pack. During hot weather they will thaw over time plan accordingly. DO NOT SUBSTITUTE FOR FREEZER PACK.

TDZ: Temperature Danger Zone 41°F-135°F: This is the optimum temperature that bacterial growth is at its highest. High protein/high moisture foods such as lamb, beef, chicken, pork seafood and any other raw meats, need to be kept below 40°F, as they are highly susceptible to bacterial regeneration in the TDZ.

Internal Cooking Temperatures: Cook Raw Meats to: lamb & beef: 145°F, raw pork 155°F, raw chicken: 165°F, ground and/or stuffed meats, burger patties, sausages: 165°F.

Vacuum packaging and Zipper Loc Baggies: Just like "As Seen on TV" a great tool used for packaging and sealing foods. The unit works by taking out (creating a vacuum) air (one of the contributors to bacterial growth) thus inhibiting or slowing down the chemical breakdown of food products and lengthening the life of the product, before sealing the bag. Foods must be completely cooled below 40°F before packaging. Vacuum Packaging is also a great way to waterproof or mud-proof items such as food, matches or even clothing. An economical way of going about this is to use zipper loc style baggies. This can also be used a means of reheating foods, sous-vide cooking, which is fancy culinary jargon for boil-in-a-bag.

Reheating Precooked Foods: Reheat precooked items to an internal temperature of 165°F to ensure safety.

Precooked items: Take caution when preparing these items at home to later be used on the trail to reheat. Make sure when preparing at home to cool the cooked items to less than 40°F within 2 – 4 hours of original preparation time.

Basic Bleach Sanitizer: for cleaning utensils and cutting boards: 1 teaspoon of bleach per 1-gallon of water. Better yet the Bleach/Sanitizer wipes you can now purchase at most supermarkets are excellent. Make sure to not use them for personal hygiene. LABEL EVERYTHING to ensure nobody drinks the bleach mixture. I can tell you from personal experience chugging a pint of that mix will have you hurling any of the wonderful food you have prepared!!!!

Wet Wipes: For use for personal hygiene when showers are not nearby.

Butane and Propane: Check all equipment connections and controls for leaks by smell, and/or rubbing a soapy water mix around connections, watch for air bubbles. Air bubbles mean there is a leak somewhere in the connection or hose. If leaks are present do not use, as this could cause serious injuries and forest fires. Remember to check local fire warnings in the area you will be camping, wheeling, and cooking in. You can call the local National Forest Service for the area you will be in for information about this, especially if you will be cooking over a campfire. Provided at the end of this book is a list of contacts for the local Colorado Forest Service.

Campfires: Check with local authorities such as the National Forest Service or Parks and Recreation Dept. for the area you will visit. Some regions require that you obtain a campfire permit.

Before Heading Out: Cooking items at home, for preparation on the trail, is a great way to avoid having to carry raw food products that tend to be more susceptible to being perishable. Everything from home drying to pre-made soups, sauces, burritos, wraps, stews and chili can all be made in any home kitchen, cooled down to less than 40°F within a 4 hour time period. Store in Ziploc bags, vacuum pack or wrap in foil then freeze. The frozen items also double as additional freezer packs in your cooler, however do not replace them entirely. Once on the trail you can either place the foil wrapped item onto a hot engine block, side of a campfire ring or in a skillet to reheat to a safe internal temperature of 165°F.

Pre-made food items vacuum packaged or in heavy duty Ziploc bags can be directly placed into a pan of boiling water (known as sous-vide cooking) or empty the contents into a pan to reheat and serve. Cooking in Foil or Ziploc Baggies saves time when it comes to cleanup.

My Jeep Grille Adventure's showcases a variety of different recipes and methods of preparation that will allow anybody to cook with confidence on the trail. Use the printable checklists and menu planner for your next adventure or misadventure.

Blank Templates for your use:

The following are templates for your use, photo copy for planning the food and beverage needs of your next adventure. Coming soon from the www.JeepGrilleAdventures.com web site will be free downloadable templates for easier accessibility and use. The following templates will include:

- Menu Planner
- Shopping List Planner/Checklist
- Camp Kitchen Checklist
- Other Basic Necessities

Free downloadable versions of all blank templates are available for your printing pleasure at www.JeepGrilleAdventures.com.

Sample Menu Planner

Meal/Day	1	2	3	4
Breakfast	Egg/Cheese Burritos	Oatmeal	Waffles	French Toast
Lunch	Club Sandwich Wraps	Garden Pasta Salad with Veggies	Quesadillas	Whole Wheat, Wild Rice and Grilled Chicken Wraps
Dinner	Dale's Pale Ale Hunt Camp Stew	Cajun Trout a la "Dadeo" (better be a good day fishing)	Sangre de Cristos Cheese steaks	Super Dawg's Spaghetti Dinner with Meat Sauce
Snacks	Chips & Salsa	Chili Roasted Pecans	Nuts, Bolts, Gears and bearings.	GORP Good ole Raisins and Peanuts

From the menu planner write out a grocery list by looking through each of the recipes and write out what items are needed. Use blank grocery list on next page for your shopping needs.

Blank templates for your use will be available as a download at:

www.JeepGrilleAdventures.com

Blank Menu Planner (printable)

Meal/Day	1	2	3	4
Breakfast				
Lunch				
Dinner				
Snacks/Beverages				

Meal/Day	1	2	3	4
Breakfast				
Lunch				
Dinner				
Snacks/Beverages				

BLANK GROCERY SHOPPING LIST PLANNER/CHECKLIST TEMPLATE:

Qty	Proteins:	Qty	Canned & Dry:
	Dairy:		
			Bread:
	Produce:		
			Beverages:

Camp Kitchen Checklists Template:

	Cooking Utensils: Spatula, Spoon, Fork, Tongs
	Cutlery: Chef's Knife, Boning Knife and Pairing Knife
	Can Opener, Wine Key/Bottle Opener
	Heat Sources: Butane, Propane, Canned Heat
	Burners/Stove: Many styles are available get one best suited to your needs. Don't try cooking for 20 on a lightweight backpackers stove.
	Pots, pans, griddles and grills as needed.
	Plates, Bowls and Cups
	Forks, Spoons and Knives
	Paper towels (cut a large roll in half works great)
	Salt and Pepper
	Basic Dry Herbs: Basil, Thyme, Oregano, Tarragon, Dill
	Basic Dry Spices: Paprika, Chile Powder, Granulated Garlic
	Other Spice Blend favorites of yours.
	Cleaning Towels/Towelette
	Ziploc baggies
	Collapsible Folding/Roll Up kitchen table
	Chairs Folding/Collapsible
	Water, ½-1 Gallon per person per day for drinking and about 1 gallon per day for cleaning/wiping etc.
	Other Beverages
	Breakfast, Lunch, Dinner, Snacks (refer to menu planner)
	Bleach Sanitizer Wipes

Other Necessities Template (cont.):

	Spare Clothing (extra shoes/socks/clothing)
	Personal Hygiene Items: Soap, Toothbrush, Toothpaste
	Tent or Tarp
	Sleeping Bags
	Small Pillow or Extra Sweatshirt to use for pillow
	Raingear
	Cold Weather Extreme Blanket (space blanket)
	Latex or Vinyl Gloves
	Bow and/or Hack Saw
	Shovel
	Flashlights
	Insect Repellent (load up on eating lots of garlic)
	Sun-block/Sunscreen
	Toilet Paper
	Matches (water/windproof)
	Trigger Lighter

The Trail Head:

"This isn't an I-70 rest stop!!!!"

Tidbits, Snacks and Other Cool Munchies

Well on our way into the wilds, whether be it forests, high desert plains or on the slick-rock trails some of the simplest of foods can appease the loudest of growling hunger pangs.

The Trail Head focuses on easy-to-prepare at home items. On the roadside, before the trail, a scenic stop on a gravel road or in the middle of a rock-crawling break, the following foods will surely satisfy any and all that encounter them.

4 States at once!!

Basic Jerky Recipe <u>Originally published: (http://www.4x4wire.com/outdoor/trailbites/jerky.htm)</u>

6 lb. Beef eye of round, top round, or other tough cut
¼ cup Liquid Smoke (THIS IS NOT THE DRIPPINGS FROM YOUR TAIL
3 cups Soy Sauce
2 oz Worcestershire
½ lb Dark Brown Sugar
1 Tbs Granulated Garlic
1 Tbs Fresh Cracked Black Pepper
*for spicier add to this mix:
3 oz Red Hot or other favorite hot sauce
4 oz BBQ sauce
1 ¼ teaspoon Creole seasoning
1 tsp Blackstrap Molasses
1 tsp Crushed Red Pepper

Slice the meat across the grain into ¼ inch slices. You can also ask your local butcher to cut some for you. Place in a non-reactive pan such as stainless steel or one of those plastic containers with the seal tight lids. Mix the rest of the ingredients until incorporated. Pour the marinade over the meat and place in refrigerator overnight. By letting it sit in the marinade overnight the acids in the soy and Worcestershire will help tenderize the tougher cuts of meat and yield a better product.

Lay the strips on a wire rack with a catch pan underneath (at this point if you wanted a spicier outcome sprinkle with extra black pepper or crushed red pepper). Place in a 175-180 degree oven for 5 hours. Take out and cool, place in zip lock baggies until trail time comes. Keep stored in a cool, dry, dark place. Thicker cuts keep refrigerated or even frozen until use. Note: For Fido, omit all the ingredients, except the beef, as they would be "ruff" on their tummies.

Baja Style Salmon Jerky
Originally published at: http://www.4x4wire.com/outdoor/trailbites/jerky.htm
4 pounds *FRESH salmon (Be aware when purchasing fresh salmon, it should not be mushy to the touch. The flesh should be firm and pinkish. Of course salmon you've caught yourself would be best and most fun if and when possible). Slice crosswise into ¼ inch slices. Set aside and keep cold.
1 oz Tequila optional
1 oz Triple Sec optional
4 oz Fresh Lime Juice
1 ½ Cup Grapefruit Juice
4 Tbs Cilantro Fresh- Minced
1 tsp Ginger Fresh- Minced
1 clove Garlic- Minced
Salt to taste
Cracked Black Pepper to taste
1 Tbs Chimayo Chili Powder to taste
1 tsp Cumin
½ tsp Coriander

Method of Preparation:

Mix the all ingredients except the pepper, chili, cumin and coriander together in a bowl. Pour this marinade over the salmon, let marinate for 3 hours. Mix the chili powder, cumin, and coriander together and set aside. Take the strips out and lay on wire rack with catch pan underneath. Sprinkle with cracked black pepper, chili powder, cumin and coriander. More if you like spicy, less if you don't. Place in a 180- degree oven until dry, about 6 hours. Pull out and cool.

*Note: Thinner slices will tend to be much drier and crisper, whereas thicker slices will produce a slightly chewier product.

This is a basic recipe where a variety of meats as well as spices can be used. Here are a few alternatives that are slightly higher in cost but make great jerky; buffalo, ostrich, venison, bluefish, mackerel, salmon, lobster, wild hog, and kangaroo.

Instead of black pepper use Cajun spices (there are many pre-made you can buy in your local supermarket), use a micro-brew as a marinade for an interesting flavor. Chimayo brand chili powder in my opinion is of the best quality and flavor.

Chili Roasted Pecans:

Originally published at: http://www.4x4wire.com/outdoor/trailbites/nuts/

Yield 3 Pounds1.5 quarts Pecans, Shelled

1 each Egg White

13 oz Granulated Sugar

3½ oz Chimayo Chili Powder

¼ Tbs Cinnamon

¼ tsp Kosher Salt

Method of Preparation

- In a bowl whip the egg whites to stiff peaks.
- Mix in the sugar, chili powder, cinnamon, and salt together add to the egg whites and mix well.
- Add the nuts to coat entirely. Place on a sheet pan lined with parchment paper.
- Bake in a preheated 350-degree oven.
- Stir often to prevent sticking. Continue to toast until most of the moisture has evaporated from the nuts.
- Remove from the oven and let cool.
- Once completely cool, place in an airtight container, label and date.

Coconut-Pineapple Glazed Macadamias:

Originally published at: http://www.4x4wire.com/outdoor/trailbites/nuts/

½ cup Coco Lopez *In your local supermarket (Sweetened Coconut Milk)

¼ cup Pineapple Juice

¼ cup Dark or Spiced Rum

2½ lbs Macadamia Nuts

8 oz Egg Whites

¼ lb Granulated Sugar

½ cup Shredded Coconut

¼ Tbs Kosher Salt

Method of Preparation

- Combine the Coco Lopez, rum and Pineapple juice in a saucepan and bring to a boil.

- Let reduce to a syrupy consistency. Set the mixture aside to cool.
- Place the nuts on a baking or sheet pan and place in a 300-degree oven until golden. Remove from oven and let cool.
- Whip egg whites to a stiff peak and add the salt add sugar.
- Combine the nuts, shredded coconut and syrup, and mix well.
- Add the egg whites to this mixture and mix well.
- Spread the mixture on a lightly oiled sheet pan and bake in 300-degree oven, stirring frequently until the moisture is absorbed.
- Take out and cool, once cooled place in airtight containers.

Nuts, Bolts, Gears, and Bearings

Originally published at http://www.4x4wire.com/outdoor/trailbites/nuts/

Yield: 18 cups (lots of mix for camping and more) 6 cups Chex Cereal

1 cup Pepita Seeds

1 cup Honey Roasted Peanuts

1 cup Goldfish, your favorite flavor

2 cups Pretzels Your favorite shape

(Pretzels are like personalities some are well rounded, some are straight and narrow, some are big and bold, and of course there are the twisted)

6 cups Cheerios

1 cup Cheese-itz

¾ cups Bacon Drippings (AKA: 10-W30)

¾ cup butter (AKA: 10-W40)

2 Tbs Worcestershire sauce

1 drop Liquid Smoke (THIS IS NOT THE DRIPPINGS FROM YOUR TAIL PIPE!!!)

1 tsp Garlic powder

1 tsp seasoned salt "Lawry's Seasoned Salt" or "Zatarain's Creole Seasoning"

2 tsp Hot Sauce

Method of Preparation:
- Over low heat melt together the butter and bacon drippings.
- Stir in the Worcestershire, garlic powder, seasoned salt and Tabasco.
- Bring to a boil and remove from the heat.
- In a large bowl mix together the nuts, cereals, seeds, Goldfish, pretzels and Cheese-itz.
- Add the seasoning mixture and toss to coat well.
- Place the mix on baking sheet pans.
- Bake at 225° for 1 ½ hour, stirring every 15 minutes.

Dried Peaches:

Originally Published at http://www.4x4wire.com/outdoor/trailbites/driedfruit

Yield 2 lbs. (slightly under-ripe peaches work best, the super ripe ones will yield just as much after you cut into them because they are so high in moisture)

2 tsp Salt and Sugar

1/2 cup Lemon juice, fresh squeezed

8 lbs Peaches- peeled, seeded, and cut into wedges

Method: Combine salt and lemon juice with 1 1/2 quarts of water. Peel and seed the peaches, slice into 1/4 inch wedges into the acidulated water. With a slotted spoon take out the peach slices and lay them on a wire rack in a single layer. Place the racks in a cold oven; turn the oven on to 130 degrees. Place something in the oven door to keep it ajar and raise the temp to 170 degrees. Let them dry for about 5 hours or until there is no moisture present. Let the fruit cool. Pack away, again do not taste test to many of these, you won't have any for camp.

Dried Cinnamon Apples:

Originally published at: http://www.4x4wire.com/outdoor/trailbites/driedfruit

How about some other fruits you say? Apples, the best varieties to use for this are McIntosh, Granny Smith, and Cortland (a McIntosh). Before cutting into your apples the first step we would take is to take two cups of water and the juice of two lemons and place in a bowl. This is so the apples will not brown as we cut slices. Wash and trim the apples of their skin-- you can skip this step if you like the skin. Slice the apple in half lengthwise and again into quarters. At this point, the core should be visible, go on and cut that core out, and slice the apple into 1/8" wedges. As you cut the slices, place them into the acidulated water, until the next step. Preheat an oven to 180 degrees. In the meantime, take the apples out of the water, toss them with just enough sugar and cinnamon to coat. Place on a wire rack or lay on parchment paper. Place that rack into the oven for 8 hours until dried. Take out of the oven, cool and set aside for the trail. Note: try not to "taste test" too many - they tend to get addictive and you won't have any for the trails.

Oven Dried Tomatoes: Yield 1 ½ cup

Originally published at http://www.4x4wire.com/outdoor/trailbites/driedfruit/

 One pound of Cherry or Roma tomatoes washed and cut in half.
Toss with enough olive oil to coat. Season with granulated garlic, fresh or dry basil, salt and pepper to taste, and mix well.
Place on a wire rack or on lightly oiled pan and put in a 180°F oven until dry. Set aside and let cool. Store in Zip-Loc bags as is or in  jars with olive oil. If you like tomatoes these make great snacking on some fresh rustic style bread with some olives. These can also be pureed in a food processor to use as a spread, especially for pizza.

Pizza Dough: makes about 3 Pizza Shells (may need to be adjusted for high altitude)

I included the pizza dough recipe under the snack category as it lends well to quick tidings, however this can just as easily be served as a lunch or dinner item.

.25 oz Yeast
1 Tbs Sugar
2.5 cups Water -- 110 Degrees
2 Tbs Olive Oil
1 Tbs Salt
6 cups Flour, (Hi-Gluten or Bread)

Method:
- Measure hot water into mixer bowl.
- Add yeast, sugar. (Let sit in a bowl for 5 minutes to activate the yeast).
- Add remaining ingredients, fit machine with dough hook and mix until well blended.
- Let mix 25 minutes on slow, then weigh out and shape.
- Spray with oil, cover and refrigerate until needed or......
- Roll out dough to desired thickness and place on hot grill (California Style) or place on cooking tray and cook until golden brown. These can be made ahead or keep raw to make at camp over an open fire grill or in a skillet.
- Top with your favorite toppings like oven dried tomatoes or oven dried tomato spread and fresh buffalo mozzarella or any cheese for that matter.

OPTIONS FOR DOUGH: Make your own hot pockets, pre-bake, cool, wrap in foil. The shell can be reheated on your engine block or in a skillet.
Get creative with the whole family this way everyone gets what they want. Also this is a great way to use up leftovers in the fridge or freezer.

OPTIONAL CHEESES: Brie, Gruyere, Emmental, Mahon and Goat Cheese to name a few.

OPTIONAL INGREDIENTS: Pepperoni, Prosciutto, Capicola, Regular Ham, Sliced Turkey, fried peppers, grilled eggplant or other grilled vegetables.
Be creative and have equal amounts of fun making and eating these.

A variety of amazing Artisan Cured meats can be found in DeNver, CO from:
Il Mondo Vecchio-Salumi Fatto a Mano
www.MondoVecchio.net

NOTES:

Early Morning or Late Morning Breakfasts:
Thinking back through the years, especially in my youthful and much more confident days when four, five, six or seven a.m. was not an option unless it revolved around fishing or hunting, even then... getting up wasn't easy....never mind making something to eat! Are you kidding me!?!

Summer of 1990 Race Point Cape Cod National Seashore, cool glasses huh?!

An early or late riser will appreciate these easy to make breakfasts that are hearty and filling...at least until lunch rolls around!

My Mom's Cape "Cahd" Special "Peppah" and Egg "Sangwiches": Serves 2 - 4
Even though I hated green bell peppers mostly due to my mom's stuffed green bell peppers...YUK!! ("Thanks Mark my son my son"!) This dish is a fond memory from my youth. For the most part Mom wasn't the greatest cook ("sorry ma I still love you"!) ("Thanks again Mark my son my son")however, the items she could cook were unforgettable! Ma would make these at home on white bread and wrap in foil... the smell of sautéed peppers and scrambled eggs still lingers in my mind's nose. Kind of like a mind's eye, rather it is what chefs have, a mind's nose...just trust me on this one!
4 Eggs Beaten
1 Large Green Bell Pepper seed, dice med
Salt and Pepper to taste
4 Pieces Wonder Bread (you can use any that is just what we used to buy all the time)
This would be great on some nice sourdough or ciabatta bread.
Method of preparation: In a non-stick skillet, heat the oil. Add the peppers to cook through until soft. Drain most of the excess oil. Add in the eggs, salt and pepper, and mix in to cover the peppers. Keep stirring until the eggs look like scrambled eggs, having covered the peppers.

Jeep Date 2006:5:23: MOAB 2006

With a great evening's sleep and no dust storms, I had a Multi-Grain Bagel with Villa Tatra's All Natural Smoked Colorado Trout www.villatatra.com for a mid morning breakfast.
1 Multi-Grain Bagel or Bagel Flavor of your Choice (toasted)
2 Tbsp Cream Cheese (Regular, Fat Free or Flavored)
1 Tbsp Capers
1 slice Red Onion
1 Leaf of Lettuce; Romaine, Bibb or Green or Red Leaf
1 - 8oz Package Villa Tatra Smoked Colorado Trout

Slice and toast the bagel halves in a skillet or over warm coals. Spread the cream cheese and place the capers in the cream cheese on one of the bagel halves. Finish with the lettuce, onion, trout, and sprinkle some lemon juice over it. Cover with the other bagel half and enjoy.

Excerpt from an Adventure with Land Rover Enthusiast Noah Gardner (former owner of Rovers North Quarterly Publication) Summer 2002: Noah Gardner/Mark DeNittis
Our first Overland trip started on a Thursday afternoon at Chef Mark's house for a

quick lunch of… what else would you expect from an Italian Chef… pasta aglio e olio (garlic and oil) and Carmine's Italian Sausage. Once lunch was finished, we began to slowly load up the Jeep, which always seems to be a task, because everybody has their own method of packing. After overcoming this first obstacle, we began our journey into the unknown and what we would face in the desert of Grand Junction.

You'll need to bear with us as this was our first trip of the summer, so there would be somewhat of a learning curve.

Due to a late arrival in Grand Junction we decided to eat our first meal at a local brewery, Rockslide Brew Pub. After quenching our thirst and quelling our hunger we headed to our fist campsite, 21 Road. 21 Road trail is not recommended for stock vehicles. We chose the spot as it is easy access and known for its fun-to-articulate rocks lending well to our mildly modified vehicles. The decision to camp there was to wake up early and play on some rocks before going into town to locate the ingredients for our menus. Too excited to wait until morning (leave it up to me to want to go wheel at night), it left the Land Rover with a broken shock mount and a frustrated driver.

As dawn rose like the desert heat, we spent the better part of morning looking for a replacement shock, bouncing from store to store until we decided to try Napa Auto, which was the least likely place (in our mind) to have an extended shock for the Land Rover. That was mistake number two, (or was it???).
We then finally made our way back into town searching for what was to become the "Grand Junction Menu".

Grand Junction Desert Breakfast Menu:
- Egg-Chorizo Rolled Tacos/Burritos
  - Mango-Laced Pancakes
- Home-style Cinnamon Raisin French Toast

Basic Breakfast Burritos

Serves 3 (Two Burritos per person)

½ lb Chorizo or Breakfast Sausage Jimmy Dean Style. (Sage Flavored or Hot are my favorites). If in the Denver area get the fresh made stuff from Carmine Lonardo's.

1 Small Onion, diced

6 Large Eggs

1 Anaheim Chile Pepper, remove seeds and pith, dice fine

Over a medium-high flame or heat source cook the sausage. Strain off excess amount of fat from sausage leaving a little (about 3 Tbs.) to cook the onions, peppers, and eggs in. Add the onions to cook until soft. Add the eggs, scramble, cook until soft. Set aside in refrigerator let cool.

2 Tbs. Oil or melted butter.

2 Potatoes Yukon Gold Washed, Shredded

Cook in butter or oil until golden brown, set aside to let cool.

½ lb Cheddar Cheese (Shredded)

6 12-inch flour tortillas

Method of Preparation:

Once all of the cooked items have cooled, you can begin assembling them. Divide all the ingredients between the 6 tortillas. Roll as in the pictures, then roll in a paper towel, and finally roll in Heavy Duty Aluminum Foil. Place in freezer until time to leave for camp. The paper towel absorbs any excess moisture to keep the burrito dry as it re heats and can be used as a napkin.

Ready for freezing and reheating later at camp or on the trail.

Note: Whole Wheat tortillas can be used, but, for some reason, the paper tends to stick to the tortilla after reheating. Quick fix…nix the paper towel and spray foil with pan spray.

Other Options:

- Cooked Sliced Steak
- Grilled, Roasted or Steamed Vegetables
- Smoked Trout or Salmon with Cream Cheese
- Chorizo Sausage
- Add a teaspoon of your favorite salsa.

Reheat the wrapped burritos to an internal temperature of 165ºF (use your culinary tire gauge). Many methods of reheating can be used while wrapped in its foil--- in a skillet over low to medium heat, engine block, over low coals, or a 12 volt-lunchbox oven (like long distance truckers use). You could also un-wrap it, but I do not recommend using the engine method of reheating.

More from Summer 2002 Adventure continued……

….being it was so warm we decided not to sleep in the tent that night. Chef Mark slept up on his roof rack and the rest of us laid out a tarp to sleep on the soft sand. In the middle of the night we awoke to a friend yelling that he saw something big moving in the bushes. After taking a quick look my friend thought that he might have been just hearing and seeing things. It was just wild desert turkeys, not the drinkable kind either. That morning came fast (mistake, not sleeping in a tent in the desert, the sun tends to be very bright and hot). As we all slowly got off of the tarp, Chef Mark had already started a kettle of cowboy coffee on the stove. We then went on the first of many river swims of that day.

As breakfast permeated the morning air, the three hungry rafters from the night before arrived to have a cup of coffee and some orange juice. While waiting for breakfast to finish, Chef Mark wanted to take the plate presentation photos. He placed the plate on a neatly stacked pile of river rock, positioned himself on the ground to take the photos.

While watering down the rocks out of the Colorado blue sky, Chef Mark darts up and starts jumping around and screaming about something going up his shorts. After a few minutes of gut busting laughter, Mark continued taking the photos then we ate breakfast. Ten or so minutes pass since he felt something crawl up his shorts. We were all standing around trying to figure out just how big and what could have possibly gone up his shorts, when all of a sudden a lizard, tail missing, falls out of his shorts, which you could imagine scared the hell out of Mark. He ran straight into the river while the rest of us just fell to the ground in a fit of laughter.

For the rest of the day nobody was willing to sit on the ground in fear of the Shorts-lizard. "The sacrifices one must make for the perfect photos"!

On our way back home to Denver they had closed I-70 just east of Rifle due to the Coal Seam Fire.

Ultimately we had to backtrack and go up to Steamboat, CO. This was an additional 170 miles or so that were not intended as part of the trip.

On the road a long time we decided it best to stay in Steamboat until morning. Coming into the home stretch into Denver on I-70 an ominous haze filled the sky…

The Greater Denver Metro Area Beginning of The Haymen Fire Blaze and Haze

…..sure enough it was another fire…the Hayman largest in Colorado history. I am sorry, excuse my East Coast attitude on this one, but the stupid dingbat that started the Hayman Fire… I'm glad got locked up. However I and many other outdoor enthusiasts are now locked out of access to that area for four wheeling, camping or fishing. It was a magnificent area. This put a damper on the original summer plans of writing this book. The format was slightly different and was going to be a collaborative effort.

Note: (Noah Gardner):The Land Rover Chef included in these efforts was former owner of Rovers North a quarterly publication for Land Rover enthusiasts. The 2002 "Summer-of-Fire" put a considerable damper on the coals for recipe excursions. However, most unfortunate was the large impact and loss to the good people residing in those areas.

Basic and Fancy French Toast

Home Style Bakery Cinnamon Raisin Bread French Toast was a hit. Make sure to stop by Home-style Bakery in Grand Junction, Colorado and ask for their special cinnamon swirl bread. The ladies were so kind as to donate this to us for our trip the summer of 2002.

2	cups Milk
1	cup Heavy Cream
6	each Eggs
1	cup Sugar
1	pinch Nutmeg
½	tsp Vanilla Extract
3	slices White or Wheat Bread

Method of Preparation:

Mix the first 6 ingredients together in a bowl with a whip to incorporate well. Heat some clarified butter on a hot griddle top.

Dip the bread in the batter and put on griddle to brown lightly on both sides. Serve whole or cut in half diagonally if using square bread.

Garnish with powdered sugar and strawberries.

Other French Toast Versions/Twists:
- For a real belly buster version make a banana-and peanut butter sandwich then dip in batter and cook....WOOOOOW!!!

Summer of 2002 Grand Junction Trip overlooking the Colorado River Basin, May Flats in Rabbit Valley

Great Side Dishes:
- Crispy Old World Thick Slice Bacon
- *Sweet Potato and Green Onion Home Fries (see Potato Hash Recipe pg. 32)

Oatmeal Breakfasts: Serves: 4-6
Buy any store-bought quick mix oatmeal, flavored or plain, heat some water and add to the oatmeal. Follow the directions on the package... how much easier can I make this one be for you?!?
Real good for the day after a late night around the campfire when cold carbonated refreshments were consumed in excess.

Hot Oatmeal Fancy Pants Style: Great for cold camping!
(Fancy.... like a Jeep with OE Air Conditioning)

2 cups Steel Cut Oats (find at your local health food store)
1 cup Favorite Dried Fruits (Cranberries, Cherries, Blueberries, Banana Chips)
1 Cup Nuts (Sliced Almonds or Walnuts)
1 Tbs Flax Seeds (these will certainly help with any blockage you may be experiencing).
Mix all dry ingredients in advance to store and carry until needed.
Add 2 cups hot boiling water to steep, soften and enjoy.

CrawlerTech4x4 and Chef Mark's Summer 2005 Meet and Greet:

Coffee Dusted Skillet Steaks, Scrambled Eggs served with Three Onion Potato Hash

Jeep Date Log 723-2405:Pickle Gulch to Kingston Peak:

http://www.4x4wire.com/feature/chefmark/summer05/

An outstanding basic, scenic trail with fun mildly challenging obstacles and lots of high elevation mountain views!

All those in attendance were along from a new local Denver shop, Crawler Tech 4x4's for a meet and greet trail ride and camp out. I hosted a great breakfast for everyone in attendance: which consisted of: Colorado's Best Beef www.cobestbeef.com Coffee Dusted Skillet Steaks, Scrambled Eggs served with Three Onion Potato Hash and steeping hot Yirgacheffe Cup o' Joe from local Aurora, Colorado's, small batch Coffea Rostir www.coffearostir.com. His award winning coffee makes for great cool morning camp conversations with the camp chef while he makes breakfast. The Coffee seasoning on the skillet steaks may sound odd, but I'll tell you it has a blend of other ingredients that lends to a sweet and savory addition to beef, especially for breakfast. Fred enjoys a good breakfast to start the day, and that is just what Chef Mark served up.

Skillet Steaks: Serves 4-8 people.

We had about 15 total people that day for breakfast.

4lbs (8oz steaks) Colorado's Best Beef All Natural 14 Day Dry Aged Shoulder Tender Steaks (any steak will do although this is typically a little cheaper and makes for a great skillet steak) An incredibly tasty and even more tender cut from the shoulder is top blade more commonly known as a "Flat Iron" or Chuck Eye Roll Steak would work well too. If you want to go for top of the line Filet Mignon, Rib Eye or NY Strips those would fill the need as well.

1 Tbs Cattleman's Grille Coffee Dust or try
7 Bar Grille's Culinary Modification Tool: Die Trying Steak Rub
(See www.7BarGrille.com for details)
Season the Steaks with the seasoning blend and sear on both sides to desired temp. I like mine "moo" rare…like there is any other way!

That day Jeremy wanted his Jeep like his breakfast eggs…OVER EASY!

Three Potato Hash:

3- Tbs Salad Oil or Crisco (bacon dripping can also be used)

1 bag frozen shredded potatoes (for ease although fresh can be used)

1 bunch (8 each) Green Onions (pre sliced at home)

1 small Yellow Onion (pre diced at home)

1 small Red Onion (pre diced at home)

In a skillet: Heat the oil and add in all the ingredients. Try not to stir too much as to allow the potatoes to brown and crisp.

- Substitute with sweet potatoes for an outstanding twist.
- This is especially yummy if cooked in bacon fat…yes I said bacon fat!
- Serve with a heaping helping of "order-up" eggs any style. If you want to take it easy serve the eggs the way you want to and they'll like what they get!

Pickle Gulch Trip Colorado Summer 2005 meet and greet hosted by CrawlerTech4x4 and Jeep Grille Adventures Camp Kitchen & Cookbook

Pancakes:

Make at home to reheat on the trail-- makes for easy cooking and cleanup.
Follow the directions on the box.
Add your favorite goodies.

- o Chocolate Chips
- o Berries
- o Diced Apple & Cinnamon

Skillet Huevos con Chorizo Pappas (Skillet Eggs atop Chorizo Hash): Serves 4 - 6

½ lb. Mexican Chorizo (store bought or go to the "barrio" carneceria to buy the real deal)
2 cups Frozen Store Brand Shredded Hash Browns
2 Tbs Green Bell Peppers Diced
9 ea Eggs
4 ea Flour Tortillas

In a skillet on medium heat melt the butter and add the onions, potatoes and peppers. Let cook for 5 minutes. Add the chorizo and mix well. Over med heat continue to cook until potatoes begin to brown. Mound little piles or nests with the chorizo hash. Crack 2-3 eggs atop each nest to cook to desired doneness.

You could scramble the whole thing together but it won't look nearly as pretty.

Lazy-man's Breakfast suggestions: Little to no cooking knowledge required.
- Frozen Waffles
- Frozen Pre Cooked Pancakes
- Frozen Egg Dishes Such as Sizzlers Frozen Meals

Whether store-bought or homemade these make for great quickies at camp. These can be wrapped in foil, be put on coals of a fire to cook, be cooked via traditional means of the propane stove in a pan, or even more classically prepared by heating with the warmth of your favorite 4, 6 or 8 cylinder engine varieties!

NOTES:

3-D Trail Moab, Utah

Most all of these recipes can be prepared at home, days prior to a trip. Simply follow them through to the end, let cool and then package for easy heating/reheating on the trail or at the campsite. If making ahead of time make sure to let the product cool before packaging into food safe containers, this will aid in the avoidance of food related illnesses.

SAFETY NOTE: Do not cover hot foods when cooling in a refrigerator or freezer, the heat will not escape and may spoil all of your hard work.

Basic Philly Cheese Steak: Serves: 4-8

1 tsp Olive Oil
2 lb Beef Sirloin – Shaved (Ask your butcher to shave or slice thin for you.)
1 small Red Onion - sliced thin
1 cup Green bell pepper - sliced thin

2 dashes Worcestershire sauce
Salt and Pepper -- to taste
4-6 slices Provolone Cheese or your favorite cheese.
4-6 ea Hoagie roll -- Toasted

Method of preparation:
- Heat oil in a skillet, griddle or sauté pan.
- Add shaved sirloin, onions, and peppers.
- Let cook, deglaze with Worcestershire sauce.
- Season with salt and pepper.
- Place provolone on top to melt.
- Place in toasted hoagie.

On the trail reheat the mix and place into your favorite bread selection.

Sangre de Cristos Cheese Steak Sandwich: Serving 4-8 Each

2 lb Sirloin Steak – Shaved (ask you local butcher to shave for you) some have pre shaved meat available as well.
¾ lb Poblano Peppers - Roasted & Cut into thin strips
1 ea Red Onion cut into thin strips

2 cups Sangre de Cristo Marinade -- ***See recipe (pg 36)
Salt And Pepper -- To Taste
12 oz Barbecue Sauce – ***See Recipe (pg. 37)
2 slices Monterey Jack Cheese
4-8 ea Hoagie Roll

Method of Preparation:
- In a hot pan heat some oil and add the shaved sirloin to sear.
- Add the onions and peppers.
- Season with the Marinade.
- Heat through and season with salt and pepper.
- On the trail reheat the mix and place into your favorite bread selection.
- Add the barbecue sauce to heat and top with cheese to melt. Place fillings into a hoagie roll or on a bun. Enjoy!

Sangre de Cristo Steak Marinade: Makes 2 cups:

1 tsp Jalapeno Pepper -- Minced
1 cup Sangria or other Fruity Red Wine
2 Tbs Cilantro Chopped Fine
½ cup Onion – Grated or minced fine

2 large Clove Garlic -- Minced
1 Tbs Olive Oil
1 tsp Cracked Black Pepper
1 tsp Cumin Ground

Method of Preparation:
- Place the first six ingredients into food processor.
- Slowly add the oil in a thin stream to emulsify until smooth.
- Adjust seasoning with cracked black pepper.

Sangre de Cristo BBQ Sauce: Makes 1 pint

1/3 cups Ketchup
1 Tbs Light Chili Powder
    (Chimayo if possible)
1 tsp Vegetable Oil
1 tsp Worcestershire Sauce
1 oz Sugar
1 oz Lemon Juice Fresh
    Squeezed
1 clove Garlic - Minced

1 small Onion -- Minced
½ cup Tomato Paste
¼ ea Diablo Beer 22 oz. – from
    Steamworks Brewery in
    Durango, CO (the other
    ¾ is for the chef of course.)
1 ea Chipotle Pepper – Seeded
    & Minced

Method of Preparation:
- Place all the ingredients in a large sauce pan, bring to a boil.
- Reduce heat to low and simmer for 1 hour; stirring occasionally.
- Make in large batches to use on a variety of items from steaks to chicken to pork.

Creamy Hill Country Potato Salad: Serves 6 - 8

2 Pounds Red Potato – boiled whole
until fork tender
½ cup   Scallion - Chopped Fine
1Tbs   Chives - Chopped Fine
1 Tbs   Parsley sprig - Chopped Fine

2 Tbs   Mayonnaise
1 tsp   Dijon or Grain mustard
1 tsp   Lemon juice -- Fresh Squeezed
Kosher salt -- to taste
Cracked black pepper -- to taste

Method of Preparation:
In large stainless steel bowl, mix all of the ingredients. Adjust seasoning with salt and pepper. Place in container and keep refrigerated until ready to serve.
Options: Add chopped cooked bacon or Bacon Bits from the grocery store.

This section of trail runs westward from the May Flats area in Rabbit Valley. It meanders along the Colorado River to a point that comes out to pavement at Westwater, UT. Caution as it runs along the railroad tracks.

Along the Colorado River about a mile or two, west of the Colorado border in Utah.

Garden Pasta Salad with Grilled Vegetables: Serves 4 - 8

2 cups	Garden Rotini Pasta -- Cooked & Cooled
½ cup	Roasted Red Peppers -- Diced
¼ cup	Green Onions -- Grilled & Chopped
½ cup	Asparagus – Grilled and Chopped
2 cups	Your Favorite store-bought Vinaigrette
3 Tbs	Fresh Parsley -- Chopped

Salt and Cracked Black Pepper -- To taste
Method of Preparation: For the salad: Toss all ingredients together in a bowl, adjust seasoning with salt and cracked black pepper. Serve in cup as side.

My wife's Cole Slaw: (reprinted with permission and having to focus more on the honey-do list and less "Jeep" breakage)! Serves: 4-8

2 cups Cabbage
1 ea medium Carrot Grated
1 small Red Onion Diced Fine
½ cup Olive Oil
1 oz White Vinegar or Apple Cider Vinegar
1 tsp Sugar
Salt & Pepper to taste
Mix all ingredients together and dig in.

Mom in-law Laura's Cucumber-Onion Yum! (Fridge Pickles)
Serves 4-8
3 ea Cucumber
1 ea Medium Red Onion slice thin
½ cup White Wine Vinegar
2 Tbs Granulated Sugar
1 tsp Kosher Salt
1 tsp Cracked Black Pepper

Mix in bowl and put in Tupperware container or Ziploc bag. Let marinate for at least one hour before eating.

Grandma's Vegetable Cole Slaw: Serves 4-8

2 cups	Cabbage -- Julienne Fine	3 Tbs Cider Vinegar
½ cup	Carrot -- Julienne Fine	1 Tbs Honey
½ cup	Red Bell Pepper -- Julienne Fine	1 Tbs Lemon Juice – Fresh Squeeze
¼ cup	Green Onion -- Chopped	2 Tbs Grated Onion
½ cup	Radishes – Chopped Fine	Salt & Cracked Black Pepper to taste
¼ cup	Celery Root -- Julienne Fine	

Method of Preparation:
- Combine the, vinegar, honey, lemon juice and onion in a bowl.
- Fold in all the julienne vegetables, adjust seasoning with salt and cracked black pepper.
- Chill and put into a food safe containers until needed.

Penne Pasta With Oven Dried Tomato-Basil Sauce: Serving Size : 4-6

16 oz Cooked Penne Pasta
3 tsp Olive Oil (pomace or pure never Extra Virgin)
1 Tbs Garlic -- Minced
1 Tbs Shallot or Onion –Minced
2 cups Oven Dried Tomatoes
4 oz White Wine

6 oz Chicken Stock
2 Tbs Basil Fresh – Chopped (substitute 2 teaspoon if dry basil)
Salt and Pepper -- To Taste
3 Tbs Parmesan Reggiano -- Grated
1 sprig fresh basil leaf for garnish.

Method of Preparation:

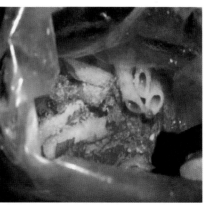

- Heat olive oil in a sauté pan.
- Add garlic and shallot to sauté 1 minute.
- Add the tomatoes.
- Deglaze with white wine and let reduce by 1/2.
- Add the chicken stock and let reduce by 1/2.
- Add in the cooked pocket.
- Season with salt and pepper.
- Add the *******chiffonade* of basil and toss. **Chiffonade fancy culinary term for thin strips.

Sprinkle with grated parmesan and garnish appropriately

Shell Pasta with White Beans and Tomato Sauce Moab Off-Road Parking Lot Pasta: Serves: 6-8 by adding beans.

Chilled and waiting for an exploded rear Dana35 to be replaced (Easter Jeep Safari 2003). Follow the pasta recipe above and add canned white beans for protein source.

Axle breakage not recommended or required.

Quesadilla With Roasted Onion and Green Chili: Serves 4-6

Originally published at
http://www.4x4wire.com/trail/cooking/recipes/

8 ea Flour Tortillas
¾ cup Yellow Onion - Small Dice
¾ cup Poblano Peppers - Roasted And Diced
4 oz Quesadilla cheese - Shredded
 Vegetable Cooking Spray

Method: (make ahead at home)

- On a hot griddle or in a skillet cook the dice vegetables until tender.
- Let cool.
- When cool, combine the vegetables, shredded cheese and herbs.
- Mix well.
- Layout 4 of the tortillas and spread the cheese mixture on each tortilla.
- Lay remaining tortillas over mix and press down lightly to seal.

At Campfire or Trail time :

- Spray both sides of the tortillas with the vegetable spray.

If cooking on the engine while on the trail, wrap in foil prior to placing on a level hot spot on engine, try not to rock crawl or get into off camber situations as this may cause loss of lunch….otherwise;

- Place the quesadilla on the grill or griddle to mark.
- Grill for 2-3 minutes or until the tortilla is golden brown.
- Flip the quesadilla over and grill until golden brown.
- Remove from the griddle and cut into wedges.

Options:

- Add pre-cooked meat or grilled chicken.
- Add refried beans or canned seasoned black beans; best for summer trips with doors off and ability to sleep with tent doors wide open.
- Roll it for ease of eating as pictured above.

An ancient depiction of a gathering of prehistoric Chef's for the feast of the beast!

Queso for Chips and Salsa: Serving Size 4-6

What camp outing wouldn't be complete without chips, queso and bean dip? You'll sure love these with cold carbonated refreshments after a day on the trail.

12 oz Queso
8 oz Heavy Cream
4 Tbs scallion -- Chopped Fine
4 Tbs jalapeno chile pepper, Minced
4 Tbs Red Onion -- Diced Fine
4 Tbs Roma Tomato -- Dice Fine
4 tsp Cilantro leaves, whole Chopped

- In a sauce pan, slowly melt the cheese over low to medium heat.
- Stir in the cream.
- Slowly stir in the onion, tomato, scallions and pepper, continue stirring until heated through.
- Stir in the cilantro.
- Let cool and put into foodsafe containers, Ziploc bags are great because you can reheat the queso by boiling the bag in water.

Borracho (drunken) Bean Dip: Serves 4-6

My very good friend and fellow chef in Houston, TX and I came up with this one. It was a favorite for many a reception at the Houstonian and Shadow Hawk Golf Courses back when we worked together. You know if it was served at a high flutin' place like that just imagine how good it'll be on the trail. When serving this you can tell all your friends around the campfire the story of how this is from a "fancy pants type place" to add to the mystique. "After hitting 18 on the private courses we strolled to the clubhouse….the Burracho Bean Dip was absolutely to die for wasn't it Lovey!" You must use a voice like Thurston Howell III from Gilligan's Island when saying this.

2.5 Tbs Bacon drippings
1 medium Red Onion - diced
3 oz fresh Jalepeno – diced (leave seeds in for spicy or take out for more mild)
1.5 cup cooked pinto beans
6 oz Beer from open 12 oz can (any type will do the other 6 oz is for the chef)
6 oz Cheddar cheese - grated
½ cup Cotija Cheese – garnish
½ cup Chopped Cilantro
Kosher salt - to taste Cracked black pepper - to taste

Method:

- Heat the bacon drippings in a pan and add the onions and jalapeños to sauté.
- Add the cooked beans and beer.
- Reduce the heat to low and add the grated cheddar and cotija.
- Cook until the ingredients are heated through and the cheese melts in.
- Take off heat to cool, stir in chopped cilantro.
- Adjust seasoning with salt and pepper.
- Let cool and put into food-safe containers, Ziploc bags are great because you can reheat the queso by boiling the bag in water.
- Serve with crisp tortillas and cheese

Carmine Jr. Italian Sausage and Pepper Sandwiches

Serves: 4 (in my case this would be all for me)
1 Loaf Fresh Italian Bread or Ciabatta
2lbs Carmine Lonardo's (Lakewood and Aurora, Colorado) Italian Hot or Mild Sausage
1 Jar Fried Peppers (found in Italian Markets as well as supermarkets Italian foods aisle)

Method: Grill the Italian sausage to an internal temperature of 165F. In a skillet heat the jarred peppers. Cut the grilled sausage into pieces and mix with the peppers. Put in bread and enjoy. Provolone or Mozzarella cheese goes well with this.

The Lonardo's have some of the best sausage around!!
(see contact information in the Contacts Section)

Serves: 6-8
The same can be served with pasta. Simply cut the cooked sausage into bite sized pieces. In a skillet toss 1 pound precooked pasta, sausage pieces and fried peppers to heat through. Serve bread on the side. Add grated Parmesan or Pecorino cheese.
Great as a lunch or dinner item.

Evening Tidings:

After a long day on the trail all one can think about is kicking back, eating a hearty meal and consuming a cold refreshing beverage. The recipes that follow are sure to make your day complete. I have, with these recipes, eaten extremely well in the middle of nowhere… often times better than in some of the restaurants I have visited and for a fourth of the cost. Of course, I always get the best seat in the house. If I can prepare these out of the back of my Jeep just think of the dinner parties you could have out of the RV camper.

Sunset dining on the Colorado Utah Border Summer 2002

More from Chefs Adventure Summer 2002:

Around 1:30pm we finally agreed on ingredients to purchase for our meals. Too many Chefs… as the saying goes holds true! Upon making our choices, we made our way onto I-70 westward to exit 2 and headed south into the Colorado Canyons of Rabbit Valley. The nice thing about this BLM land was the presence of maps located along the trail, so it was impossible to get lost. We followed the "Kokopeli" trail meandering through some scenic desert landscapes with reddish-light khaki slick rock cliffs and other rock formations. Little before trail's end, we took a detour over a cattle grate and unknowingly headed into Utah. As we zigzagged our way down to the Colorado River, we ended up next to a railroad crossing… this area, as it turns out to be, is known as May Flats. We crossed the tracks and made a bee-line straight for the river, parked, jumped out and didn't stop until we were waste deep in refreshing water. After taking a quick dip and recovering some of our sanity, we realized that we were in Utah. This was originally supposed to be a Colorado camping cookbook. After a few minutes of discussion and joking around about our quandary, the first words out of Dave's mouth

as he was getting out of the water were, "I think there's a better camp site down the river!" So began the impossible… finding the perfect campsite. Doing some mild brain damage, we eventually solved the campsite problem. Once again, a quick dip back into the river to make sure it was a suitable swimming area, "remember I told you that it was hot out there and you always need a good swimming hole in the desert".

Unpacking the roof racks, I heard Chef Mark say, "Look up there on the cliff, we are in Colorado", painted in white on the red cliff just north of the river was "Utah/Colorado" border line, we sat about 20 feet on Colorado side. Finally things were looking good, camp as set up, the sun was setting, everybody was hungry, and it was time to cook. While preparing dinner, we noticed three rafters camping down the way, so we took a stroll down to their camp and invited them over for supper, which they gladly accepted

Cilantro-Lime Pork Barbacoa

4 lbs Country Style Pork Ribs
1-cups Olive Oil
6 ea Limes, Juiced
1 bunch Cilantro, chopped fine
5 cloves Garlic (Great natural Mosquito repellent)
1 Jalapeno diced fine
Salt and Pepper - to taste
Toss all the ingredients together, and pour marinade over the ribs to coat well. Let sit for a minimum of an hour in your cooler. Over a hot grill, cook the ribs until an internal temperature of 155 or about 8 minutes on each side. The longer the pork is in the marinade, the more intense the flavor.
Goat Cheese Rajas Au Gratin
4 ea Red Potatoes, sliced thin
½ White Onion, sliced thin
3 Poblano Chilies roasted
½ to 1 cup Goat cheese (as much as desired)
Butter.

Method of Preparation:
First roast the chilies, until they are all black, then place them back into the plastic bag to "sweat" for about 8 minutes. Peel off the blistered/burnt skin, de-seed and cut into thin strips. Meanwhile, slice the potatoes and onion and then place the potatoes on a piece of tin foil. Add the onions, poblano peppers, some butter and goat cheese. Wrap the foil around the potatoes. Place the package on top of the grill and let cook for about 10 minutes until fork tender. Season to taste

Tomatillio Salsa Verde

12 ea Tomatillos, rinsed and husked
½ White Onion, small dice
4 Tbs Cilantro (hand full)
4 cloves Garlic, smashed
2 ea Limes
3 Poblano peppers, seed & dice
Salt and Pepper - to taste
Grind to a chunky consistency in a mortar and pestle, otherwise puree in a blender.

Breaking in a new mortar and pestle.

TIPS:
- Before placing marinated products on a grill be sure to shake off excessive oil, as it will cause flames, and the smoke of those flames will give the product a carbon-like, off flavor.
- Finely ground desert sand is not a required ingredient, but you may get dashes of it as the wind blows.

Dale's Pale Ale Hunt Camp Stew: Serves 2-4

Originally published at http://www.4x4wire.com/outdoor/trailbites/hunt_camp/

www.oskarblues.com

"A Huge Voluminously Hoppy Mutha of a Pale Ale" as quoted on this canned Rocky Mountain Pale Ale made at Oskar Blues Brewery in Lyons, Colorado, is used to make this hearty and FLAVORFUL stew. Although this stew can be made at home and typically stews are better the second time around "Encore Presentations", I chose to pre cut all the ingredients at home to be able to prepare this dish at camp. Although not in the first attempt as can be seen in the (upcoming) pictures, I have incorporated sour cream into the recipe. This mellows some of the heat from the black pepper and HOPPY flavor of the beer. This dish is very similar to the Hungarian "porkolt" (goulash style) known as Tokany, a goulash style stew, but, instead of paprika, black pepper is the main spice. A plus for black pepper fans, and it warms the soul on cold late fall hunt trips. Dale's Pale Ale registers in at 6.5% alc by volume. Any flatlanders coming out to the high-country elevations be cautious… this beer will "bite you in the boo-boo" to say the least.

IMPORTANT NOTE: The recipe calls for 3 cans of Dale's Pale Ale… please realize one can is for the stew, one for during cooking to add flavor to the camp chef and one to enjoy the meal with.

On a more serious note… this is, of course, after all ammunition has been removed from all firearms. Be responsible: loaded guns and alcoholic beverages DO NOT MIX!!!!!

1 Tbs Cooking Oil
1 lb. Beef Stew Meat
3 Cloves Garlic, peel and slice.
1 Small Onion, Peel and dice ½"
1-2 Tablespoons Black Pepper
3 Cans Dale's Pale Ale (seriously Hoppy….no joke) if you do not like such intense flavor any beer can be used.

8 Oz. Water
1 Med Carrot Peel and slice ¼" thick
1 Med-Large Yukon Gold or Red Bliss Potato; wash and dice into ½" cubes. Leave the skin on for nutrients and presentation.
½ Cup Sour Cream
Kosher Salt to taste

Method of Preparation: (If making at home in advance of the trip let the mixture cool and portion into Zip Loc bags).

Heat the oil in a skillet over medium - high heat. Season the meat lightly with salt and pepper and place into hot skillet. Brown all the meat and add the garlic, onions and black pepper. Let cook until the onions and garlic are soft. Deglaze (fancy chef lingo meaning add the beer) the skillet with the can of Dale's while tilting and sipping from the other can. Add the water. Bring to a boil and then reduce to let simmer for 45 minutes to one hour over low heat. Stir occasionally and tilt and sip from the other can to adequately flavor the camp chef. This will allow the meat to become fork tender and the chef to mellow, relax and take in the great outdoors. Once the meat has become fork tender add in the carrots and potatoes to cook until fork tender, for another 10 – 15 minutes. Add more water or beer if it has reduced too much. The sauce should have a semi-smooth consistency. To finish, slowly stir in the sour cream adding in 1/3 of the total amount at a time. This tempering step allows for the sauce to become smooth and creamy. Adding in cold sour cream in one big "glop" to a hot liquid may coddle the sour cream and make the sauce gritty.

Let simmer to allow the sauce to incorporate flavors and come to a creamy texture. Adjust the taste with salt as needed. Dig in, while occasionally tilting and sipping the third and final beer with your free hand!!!

High-Country American Lamb "deconstructed" Shepherds Pie with Smashed Yukon Gold Potato and Root Vegetables

Ahhhh… American Lamb, easy to use, succulent flavors, and one of my daughter's favorite dishes… actually she likes American Lamb prepared a multitude of ways. This is a great make-ahead dish when cooler weather is expected. A traditional recipe presented with a little different flair, just think of the unsuspecting folks waiting to eat a plain 'ol shepherds pie. Find more exciting recipes at www.americanlambboard.com
Serves: 4-6 each

1 Tbs Clarified Butter
4 oz Pearl Onions
1 tsp All Purpose Flour
1.5 lb American Lamb Stew Meat (1/2" dice) or Ground American Lamb
Can also substitute with 3lbs American Lamb Breast Riblets:
1 tsp Garlic Clove Sliced
4 oz Corn Kernels
4 oz Sweet Peas
4 oz. Red Wine (Syrah or Pinot Noir)
16 oz Lamb Stock or other canned stock available

For the Smashed Root Vegetables:
2 Each Yukon Gold Potatoes
3 Each Parsnips
2 Each Turnips
2 Tbs. Whole Butter
1 Tbs. Heavy Cream
Salt and Pepper to taste.
Chopped Parsley

Method of Preparation:
Start the root vegetables in a pot of cold water and bring to a boil to cook through. Strain, let dry and place in bowl. Add the milk, whole butter and season with salt and pepper.
Smash to chunky consistency. Set aside until ready to serve.
Toss the lamb in flour to lightly coat the meat, heat the butter and add the lamb to brown. Once browned take the meat out of the pan and add the pearl onions and cook until tender. Add the garlic, sweat until soft. Add the wine and let simmer for 2 minutes. Add the lamb stock, onions and lamb meat back to the pot and let simmer until thickened to coat the back of a spoon.
Adjust seasonings with salt and pepper. Assemble on a plate to serve with the smashed root vegetables or can be assembled as a traditional shepherds pie such as in a casserole. Garnish with chopped parsley.

JEEP LOG DATE: 2006:5:23 Skillet Seared Flank steak with Corn on the Cobb atop festive Brown Rice Serves 2-4

Onward to a new trail for me, that can be found north-east of Moab, known as 3-D. It starts off very easy through a sandy canyon and onto a steep loose rock hill climb before entering small domes atop a cliff with bountiful views. I found this to be a fun, mildly challenging and extremely scenic trail for a modified/built vehicle.

A final hill climb with small step at the top makes for a white knuckle moment, I of course, was unable to take a photo of that as I was alone when doing the trail. After a long day on the rock, I was hungry for a hearty dinner of good beef, rice and corn. This is what I came up with, 3-D presentation optional. The presentation is reflective of what I experienced on the 3-D trail as a whole…a Chef's perspective! Compare the photos and you be the judge! The inspiration, the raw ingredients and the piece de résistance!!

1 ea Flank Steak (approx 1.5 lb) or Flat Iron (or ask your butcher for top blade steaks) Colorado's Best Beef preferably.
Your Favorite Steak Seasoning: (try any of the 7 Bar Grille Culinary Modification Tools)
1 Tbs Vegetable Oil or Pan Spray
2 ea Corn on the Cobb, Cut in Half Diagonally (for visual appeal)
1 cup Pre-Cooked Brown Rice, mixed with ¼ cup Diced Bell Peppers.
Season steak and sear in skillet on both sides.
Cook until desired temperature is reached.
Note regarding basic cook temperatures:
If you like it MOOOING or, as they call it in the industry Black and Blue, seared one side and serve with raw cold center. Pittsburg Style, sear lightly on both sides and serve with cold red center. More information listed in safety section.
Once cooked to your liking, hopefully not well done, set aside to rest for 5 minutes before slicing. Make sure to slice against the grain, on an angle and no more than ¼ inch thick for best results.
**In a separate heated skillet, place oil or pan spray, to brown the corn on all sides. Set corn to the sides of the pan and place cooked rice blend to heat through.
Serve steak slices with rice and corn.

Moab Asian Style Alaskan Cod (when the big quake hits I just might be able to catch cod in Moab) with Veggies and Noodles: Serves 2-4

It had been 3 years since my last trip to the Mecca and since I missed hunting season last fall I deemed it a necessity for a Moab adventure. With some upgrades to the drivetrain, a Ford 8.8 in the rear and recently installed Aussie Locker, I felt confident with a newly acquired trailer in tow… thanks to Josh at Crawler Tech 4x4 in Denver. The trailer also has a unique history to it as it had hauled rock up the Holy Cross Trail just north of Leadville, Colorado, in 2000 to fix various spots en route to the "The City". The trailer has a CJ axle, with locking hubs (great conversation piece obviously not functional), 2.5 inch Rancho Springs, and 32 inch BFG MT's.

8 oz Frozen Cod (a variety of other fish can be used) let thaw before cooking.
1 Tbs sesame oil or vegetable oil
1 clove Garlic, sliced thin
4 ea Scallions, sliced 1-2 inch long
1 Carrot, Vichy Cut (fancy for sliced thin diagonally)

½ cup Broccoli Florets (frozen or fresh)
¼ cup Red Bell Pepper cut into strips
½ ea Lemon, juiced
1 tsp or Packet (like the ones you get from ordering take out) Soy Sauce
1 packet favorite Ramen (or like brand) Noodles (**see note about flavor packet)

Optional Condiment: Sambal Chili Paste, a very spicy Asian condiment found in most markets.

Method of Preparation:

In a separate pan heat up enough water, to follow the directions for the noodle packet, this usually takes only three to four minutes to cook. Plan accordingly. Strain out all of the water, to eat more like a noodle rather than a soup, as its intended purpose. **VERY IMPORTANT**: Omit at least ½ if not ¾ of the seasoning packet when straining out all the water, otherwise it may be too salty.

In a skillet (preferably non-stick for easy clean-up), heat up the oil over medium heat. Add the thawed cod to the pan with the oil to sear until golden brown on one side. Turn the cod to let cook through, until it flakes easily. Take out the cod and set aside. Add the garlic and vegetables to cook through until tender.

Sprinkle the lemon juice and soy sauce over the contents; immediately add the pieces of cod back to the pan to help warm. Let simmer for 1 minute.

Serve over the LIGHTLY seasoned ramen noodles.

Cajun Skillet Trout a la Dad-eo: Originally published at
Jeep Date Log 0730 - 80105: Bill Moore Lake Family Weekend
http://www.4x4wire.com/feature/chefmark/summer05/

From fresh mountain stream to skillet....like bein' in da bayou but at 11,000 feet above 'dem!.

Just after leaving the 1-70 corridor, about 40 miles west of Denver, is the quaint blink-and-you-might-pass-it town, of Empire, Colorado. In the center of town take a right, and you'll encounter switchbacks up to some varying levels of scenic off-roading and camping on the eastern slope of the Continental Divide.

Heading to the top by Bill Moore Lake trail, you can find loose gravel, steep hill climbs. Be alert and respectful to the mud pit being closed due to trail abuse. The Empire Loop Trail is moderate, tight in the trees in some spots and has challenging terrain for stock or mildly modified vehicles. Another direction leads to Red Elephant Hill, a scenic decent that gets challenging in two spots in particular. Two obstacles of which are steep and off camber with a drop off to one side are the most challenging. Needed is a strong sense of confidence, carefully chosen lines, light pedal work and low gears. Other than the two obstacles this can be considered a moderate trail for some and terrifying trail for others.

Going down is challenging and going up would certainly be more difficult. The trail, if heading down, brings you back to I-70 just east of the Empire exit. The beauty of the whole area, besides being alongside the Continental Divide, is the trail system diversity and close proximity of them all. Explore from a base camp over a weekend or put in a day trip of wheeling within an hour's drive from Denver. A friend from the Rocky Mountain X-terra Club joined us for a quick day trip of wheeling the area. He had only been up the lake trail previously, so exploring the two others made for a great day.

I often will make everything, when camping out, for us to eat, however, we always set aside room for a Hot Dog at Jenny's in the center of town. They have this huge Hot Dog on a huge bun with (well, my favorite) a mile high pile of sauerkraut. **Warning: I recommend eating this on the way back down from a weekend of camping. Sauerkraut has the potential effect to make for a yellow or red warning on the

bio-terror alert scale. It may trigger biological warfare system sensors from NORAD in Colorado Springs. If so, travel with doors off the Jeep to allow any biological vapors to be adequately dispersed. We did catch and cook up some fresh trout from Mill Creek at the northern section of the Empire Loop Trail.

2 ea fresh caught Trout	3 Tbs butter or Crisco
*Swamp Stompin' Cajun Blackening	
Seasoning (to your taste)	

Clean the innards from the stomach and cut off the heads. Rinse thoroughly with fresh water.

Season the Trout liberally with Blackening Seasoning. In a cast iron skillet heat the butter or Crisco. Place the seasoned trout in the skillet and let cook 8-10 minutes over medium heat on each side.

Cooking time of course would depend on how thick or big the trout is. It may be easier to cut the trout into fillets for quicker cooking time.

We didn't think we were going to stay an extra night so I didn't plan to make dinner as part of the trip. We served a magnificent old staple as a side dish…Ramen Noodles acquired from the Empire Gas Station. It made for an excellent dinner. What would've done it justice is my Cajun Dirty Rice.

"Continental" (as in Divide) Cajun Country Dirty Rice Serves 4-6

I hope one day Chef John Folse will take me up on my offer to visit Colorado, I'll take him up on the trails to enjoy this dish made with his bayou goodies at 11 or 12, 000 feet above sea level. Much different than wheeling around the bayou backcountry "fo-sho"!

1 Tbs Cooking Oil

¼ lb *John Folse and Company Andoullie Sausage* Diced Small

¼ lb *John Folse and Company Tasso Ham* Diced Small

4 cloves Garlic chopped

1 small Onion, diced small

1 stalk Celery, diced small

1 cup Converted Rice

2 cups canned or Fresh Made Chicken Broth

12 oz Fresh Cooked Chicken from Making Broth or Premium Chunk Tyson Cooked Packaged recipe ready Chicken.

*Optional 4 Oz. Cooked Tidi Shrimp in addition to the chicken

1 – 5 dashes of Tabasco

3 Each Scallions or Green Onions, chopped

¼ cup diced Green & Red Bell Pepper

1 Tbs fresh Chopped Parsley

1 pinch Cayenne

Shouldn't need additional salt or pepper as the John Folse Andoullie and Tasso will add all the flavor this dish needs.

Method of Preparation at Home

I wanted to try the new packaged cooked Tyson Chicken product as it can pack in and out easily. I found the taste to be surprisingly good. The preservatives and high sodium may not be the best but I'll take that any day over trying to deal with Salmonella poisoning. If treated properly what works best is the meat from making the chicken stock recipe mentioned later in the Extras Section of this book. Low sodium, no preservatives and fresh made what more could one ask for. In a heavy bottom pan heat the oil and cook the Andoullie and Tasso to extract the flavor. Add in the garlic, onions and celery to cook until soft. Add in the rice, and let it absorb the oils by stirring. Add in the water or chicken broth. Stir, bring to a boil, reduce to simmer and let cook covered until all the liquid has been absorbed and the rice fluffs with a fork. Take off the heat and place in a bowl, mix in the chicken (optional Shrimp), Tabasco, scallions, peppers, chopped parsley and cayenne. Adjust seasoning with salt and pepper. Let cool and then package in Zip Loc bags and freeze until needed. *Any andoullie or tasso ham can be used but Chef Folse has the best. On the Trail: Place bag in pot of boiling water until heated through.

Fourth of July Feast in the Backcountry

4th of July weekend in 2006 we arrived at our 9500 feet above sea level camp spot. That evening we had a feast. Our antipasto was a fine selection of cheeses, grapes and olives. This is the second year a few colleagues (fancy term people in education use for friends) and our families have made this trek to the Grand County area for the Fourth of July as they have a great "good 'ol fashion" time with parades and the like.

A future food stylist in the making!? This is the same exact spot on Mulstay Jeep Trail north of Granby Colorado where I set up hunt camp.

Nicoise Olives, Sicilian, Olives, Marinated Cipolini Onions, Morbier Cheese, Green Grapes and of Course Fermented Crushed White Grapes, Sesame Crackers and Grissini

Fourth of July Surf and Turf with Firecracker Diavolo Gnocchi and Grilled Asparagus: Serves 4 – 6

Originally published at http://www.4x4wire.com/feature/chefmark/summer05/

For The Gnocchi

1 - 1lb Package Gnocchi

1 qt Boiling Water

1 cup *Tomato Sauce, (use the recipe pg 40 or use your favorite from a jar).

1 – 5 pinches Crushed Red Pepper Flakes (if it's hot going in, you bet it's hot coming out!)

Follow the directions on the gnocchi package to cook. In the meantime heat the tomato sauce with some spicy red pepper flakes. When the gnocchi is finished, toss in tomato sauce. Serve with…………..

The Turf:

1 Tbs Olive Oil

4 ea Flat Iron Steaks (4-8 oz each)

1 Pkg. IQF Scallops (Individually Quick Frozen) Get at grocery store

Pinch Granulated Garlic

Salt & Pepper to taste

Coat the steaks with the olive oil season with salt, pepper and granulated garlic.

Grill the steaks to your liking over hot flames or sear in a cast iron skillet. Can slice to serve or serve the whole steak topped with scallops.

*Steaks can be seasoned and oiled in advance at home. Add some rosemary or other herbs for an interesting twist.

The Surf:

12 oz IQF Scallops

1 tsp Butter

1 Tbs. White Wine

Salt & Pepper To taste

In a skillet heat the butter to melt. Add the scallops to sauté. Deglaze with the white wine let cook for one minute. Add 1 tsp chilled whole butter; Monte au Burre "to lift the sauce". Cook until a cream-like consistency is achieved serve over the steaks.

Asparagus:

1 Tbs Olive Oil

1 tsp Balsamic Vinegar

1 bunch Asparagus (small – med)

Salt & Pepper - to taste

Toss the Asparagus in the oil and vinegar. Season with salt and pepper, grill or cook in a skillet.

So…you say you have children along for the trip, and they don't like asparagus, never mind regular vegetables… use another veggie for the kiddies. I am very fortunate that my daughter likes asparagus, however she only likes the tips…talk about a distinguished palate… must be a chef's kiddo!?

The joys of being a kid a July 4th parade, free candy and thoughts of asparagus tips.

A Holy (not the last supper) Cross Feast: Summer 2006

I didn't have to cook much this evening as my friend Josh Lowenstien (Super Dawg) of www.CrawlerTech4x4.com & www.CraneHiClearance.com gave up the wrenches and took the spatula and tongs to hand. We had a group of at least 10 folks. I provided the appetizer, Josh did the spaghetti and meat sauce, and Steve Rumore and the Rumore family of Avalanche Engineering the father of the rock buggy craze, provided the salad fixins'.

The evening's menu:
Whole Wheat Tortilla Wraps with Wild Rice, Thin Green Beans and Grilled Chicken
Spaghetti and Meat Sauce
Avalanche Engineered Mixed Greens Salad

The Holy Cross Grande Buffet

Grilled Chicken Wraps: Serves 6-8

1 Uncle Bens Wild Rice Packet (follow instructions)
1 Packet Grilled Chicken Strips (from your local grocery supermarket)
1 each 8 oz bag Frozen Thin Green Beans (from the freezer section of supermarket)
4 each Whole Wheat Tortillas
Cook and cool the rice. Layout the tortillas and distribute even amounts of the other ingredients amongst them.
Roll like a burrito. Wrap in foil. Freeze for use later on the trail. Cook by laying the wrap on hot engine while wheeling or put in skillet to cook through until 165 degrees or steaming hot if you forgot your thermometer.
The chicken legs featured in the picture were not used in this recipe.

Super Dawg's Super Duper Spaghetti

Servings: A whack-load of hungry off-road families.

2 Pounds Ground Beef
1 tablespoon Dry Oregano and Dry Basil (or just use the Italian Herb Blend most stores sell).
2 ea. Big Jars of Tomato Sauce (use your favorite kind) 1 jar is for the beef and the other is on hand just in case of non-meat eaters? HUH… people that don't eat meat!?!?…oh well, more meat for me!
2lb Spaghetti Dry
Method of Prep:
In a heavy bottomed skillet brown the ground beef and season with Granulated Garlic, Black Pepper and Salt.
Add dry basil and dry oregano.
Add 1 jar of tomato sauce let simmer for 30 minutes.
Boil 3 Gallons of water to cook pasta. Cook and drain pasta. Serve.

Avalanche Engineered Salad:

Everybody loves Rose!
The Avalanche Engineering family happened to be at the Holy Cross area that weekend playing around with a French-fry oil puffing Hummer (bio diesel). Super Dawg and the the Rumore family go back a ways, so he invited them up for some grub, they brought the salad goodies.

2 Bags of Mixed Greens and ¼ cup grated carrots, ¼ cup pumpkin and sunflower seeds, ¼ cup sliced onions and your favorite dressing.
The Rumore kitchen crew brought great raspberry vinaigrette from an organic store in Durango.
Directions: Mix, add dressing and eat.

Seared Southwestern Pork Tenderloin with Grilled Corn and Potato-Posole Green Chile

These were taken from one of my very first outdoor food photo shoots in 2001 in the area known as Hackett Gulch along the South Platte River, in Pike National Forest. Yes, that is the very area that has since been closed due to some whacked out Forest Service person who couldn't deal with her emotions and then set the whole area ablaze... to later be known as the Hayman Fire of 2002. I don't harbor much frustration towards it....well maybe just a little.

On another note, the area, I hear, has been in strong environmental recovery with the help of the Colorado Upper South Platte Preservation teams adding tremendous efforts to the recovery of this area. I think back to this trip to make this dish. It was a great scenic trail for me at the time with my mildly modified un-lifted Jeep. I really hope it re-opens soon; it is within close proximity to Denver, and the camping and fishing were awesome.

I look forward to once again visiting that location one day, and when I do, while basking in the sun, listening to the soothing flow of the South Platte, I will think fondly (here goes getting my "Mass-on") of the Forest Service dingbat sitting quietly in her prison cell, hoping she has come to terms with her "emotions" after screwing up the emotions of so many living in that area that ended up losing so much! Oh, yeah, here's the recipe for 2-4 servings:

1 Tbs Olive Oil
1- 4oz Can Green Chiles
1 Tbs Onion, Chopped
2 ea cloves Garlic, Minced
4 ea Red Potatoes, Cut into wedges or pieces.
Salt and Pepper - to Taste

8 oz Chicken Broth* (canned is fine, unless you want to make chicken stock from scratch.....recipe provided though, page 63, Extras and Upgrades section, if ya do!)
1 ea Lime cut into wedges.
1 Tbs Cilantro Chopped

- In a skillet, heat the oil and add the potatoes cook until they begin to brown.
- Add in the onions and garlic to cook through. Add the green chilies and the broth. Let simmer until liquid is reduced to half. Adjust seasoning with salt and pepper.
- Serve... sprinkle cilantro over the top and squeeze lime juice on it. YUM!!

Again this can be made ahead of time and reheated on the trail.

2 Ears of Colorado Sweet Corn Roasted in the husk.

Grill until kernels are softened. The corn can also be cut and tossed into the stew.

The Pork Tenderloin:

1 Tbs Oil Olive

1 ea large Pork Tenderloin

2 Tablespoons Southwest Blackening Seasoning

- Rub the tenderloin with the oil.
- Rub in the seasoning.
- Sear and cook to an internal temperature of 145 degrees F.

Option: 7 Bar Grille Culinary Modification Tool: Las Cruces Chile Challenge www.7BarGrille.com

Painted Desert Churrascos (grilled meats) Serves 4

These are great and any meat can be used. Skewer, grill, serve and enjoy. I find this to be particularly great using American Lamb Top or Bottom round strips or 1 inch cubes like K-Bobs.

2 lb Boneless Meat; Lamb, Chicken, Pork, Beef (do a mix, like the diverse terrain of the west)

½ Cup Painted Desert Wet Rub** See Recipe pg. 65 in Extras and Upgrades Section

Rub the seasoning into the meat. If using multiple meats, keep each separate.

Let absorb flavor for at least 2 hours. Grill to safe internal temperature.

Serve with Chimmi Churri Sauce*See Recipe page 65 Extras and Upgrades Section

Eat and enjoy. This is great with simple white rice or even wrapped in a tortilla.

This is how I served them at a reception in Scottsdale, AZ:

American Lamb Churrascos Skewered with Sugarcane, served with Mango-Agave Nectar, Tequilla Sunrise, Prickly Pear Syrup with Napolito Cactus and Kumquat.

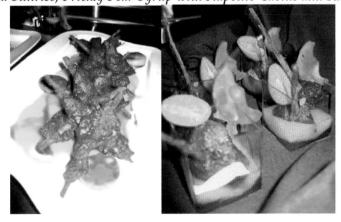

Email rmte5280@jeepgrilleadventures.com for the Mango-Agave Nectar Tequilla Sunrise, and Prickly Pear Syrup recipe.

BEVERAGES

When it is just plain hot out and simple water won't do. This recipe from a REALLY "fancy-dancy" type place in the South will certainly hit the spot and turn simple water into a citrusy favorite.

Home-style, Lemonade... that, cool refreshing drink!

Yields: 12 - 8oz. servings

9 ea Lemons, halved

2 ea Limes, halved

1 cup Sugar

¾ gallon Water - Throttle it up and replace the water with club soda/soda water.

Method of Preparation:

Juice the lemons and limes into a non-reactive container.

Add in water and sugar.

Stir vigorously to incorporate.

Let sit over night to let flavors meld.

Add other for adult version.

- Vodka
- Whiskey for a southern touch
- Rum and mint for an Island touch

Hot Cocoa

For cooler than normal snowy Rocky Mountain August camp nights

Yes snow in July or August is one of the unique aspects of living and camping in the Colorado high country.

1 Packet of You favorite Hot Cocoa Mix, Mini Marshmallows Optional

Hot Water

Adult Friendly Version

- Add Peppermint Schnapps

Option: Use 7 Bar Grille's Culinary Modification Tool: Mountain Man Cocoa with Ancho Essence www.7BarGrille.com

Hot Apple Cider

Follow packet instructions

Adult Friendly Version

- Add Jack Daniels
- Add Southern Comfort
- Add Maker's Mark

Option: Use 7 Bar Grille Culinary Modification Tool: Killington's Killah Cider Spice to mull your cider and give it the oomph it needs to be "Whicked Killah"! www.7BarGrille.com

Cowboy Coffee

Just like out on the open range.

2 Tbs Coffea Rostir Coffee www.coffearostir.com (your favorite blend or type)

1 Eggshell

1 -2 cups Water (depends on how strong a coffee you like)

Place all into a campfire coffee pot. Bring to boil. Serve. There are also many neat coffee tools at your local sporting goods store such as a French press for YUMMY morning coffee. Watching the sun rise, the fog lift, the dew on the plants, sipping on a hot cup of java….can it get any better?

My wife's Sangria: Great for hot summer days at the campsite.
Yield 6-8 servings; publishing this recipe gets me out of the dog house for a little bit.
2 large Oranges, one juiced, one cut into slices.
1 large lemon, washed and sliced
¼ th cup sugar
¼ th cup Triple Sec
1 each 750 milliliter bottle inexpensive, fruity red wine, the screw top type.
Mix all the ingredients well. Pour over ice in tall glasses, Solo Cups for the Trail or those fancy hard plastic ones work to. Enjoy on hot evenings or afternoons relaxing by the campfire.

View from a stop on Flat Iron Mesa Trail south of Moab. This place sure could use a drink!

Mama's (code for my wife) Magic No-Frills Mojitos
1 Can of Frozen Lime Ade (found in grocery store freezer sections)
5 Sprigs of Fresh Mint (leaves only)
Muddle the Lime Ade and Mint Leaves (mash it together)
½ litre of White Rum
1 litre of Soda water
Mix all the ingredients together and serve over ice.

The fresh mint can become a fun part of this campfire beverage, smile and count the mint leaves in your friend's mouth. Of course if the friend is more of a significant, intimate nature, a more fun version can be played… just use your imagination!

Summer Watermelon Punch: Yield more than ½ gallon.

1 large watermelon

2 qt lemonade (use the home-style for this)

2 cups watermelon chunks

Crushed ice

Method of prep:

Cut a thick slice of watermelon. Scoop out 2 cups of melon chunks. Press the remaining watermelon meat through a fine mesh strainer or cheesecloth, until there is 2 cups of juice. Combine juice, chunks and lemonade and chill.

Adult Friendly Versions:

- Melon liquor
- Vodka.

Caution drinking before and/or during driving is dangerous and illegal!
This is what can result because of DWUI, don't be dumb!

Actually this guy was attempting a mind over matter trick, "I think I can…I think I can, I know I can… I know I can!"

No one was hurt in the above stunt and alcohol was definitely not part of this in any way shape or form… it was completely intentional. The vehicles were back on all fours with driver skill and technique.

Tierra Del Sol 2001

NOTES:

Mango's Nebraska Peanut Corn Krisp Bars
1 cup Brown Sugar
1 cup Light Corn Syrup
½ cup Peanut Butter
5 cups Rice Krispies
Cook syrup and sugar for 30 seconds on low-medium. Stir in the peanut butter and cereal. Drop by tablespoon onto wax paper on a cookie pan. Refrigerate, wrap and enjoy on the trail.

Buffalo Chips: Yield: About 3 dozen 6-inch cookies
My first western experience as a chef was interesting, coming from the sunny shores of sea level south Florida, baking at altitude was a challenge. I found the local Grand County Colorado Chamber of Commerce Women's Club cookbook to enhance my lack of baking skill. One my favorites, as was the guests of the ranch, were these buffalo chip cookies. They literally look like big old cow patties.

1 cup Sweet Butter, unsalted, softened	2 tsp Baking soda
1 cup Shortening	2 tsp Baking powder
2 cup Brown sugar	1 tsp Salt
2 cup Granulated sugar	2 cup Old Fashioned Oats
4 lg Eggs	2 cup Corn Flakes
2 tsp Vanilla	2 cup Chocolate Chips Semi Sweet
4 cup All-Purpose flour	1 cup Flaked Coconut
	1 cup Pecans, chopped

Method:
Cream butter and shortening at medium speed. Add in brown sugar and granulated sugar, until light and fluffy. Beat in eggs, one at a time until fluffy add in the vanilla. Sift together the flour, baking soda, salt and baking powder. . Mix into creamed mixture, half at a time.
Stir in oats, corn flakes, chips, coconut and pecans.
Drop large spoonful onto cookie sheet using an ice cream scoop well spaced. Bake in 350 degree oven. 15-18 minutes for large cookies, or 10-12 minutes for smaller cookies. Can be stored frozen until needed, either the raw batter to thaw and cook at a future date or the finished cooked cooking

Pistachio Nut Brittle: Yields 8 servings

4 cups Sugar
2 cups Light Corn Syrup
1 cup Water
4 cups Pistachios, Shelled
4 Tbs Butter
1tsp Vanilla Extract
2 tsp Baking Soda

Method of Preparation
In a heavy bottom saucepan, combine the sugar, syrup and water.
Bring to a boil cook until semi thick beyond syrupy stage. Like thick gear lube.
Turn heat to low and add the nuts. Simmer until almost very thick.
Remove from the heat and fold in the butter, vanilla and baking soda.
Mix well and pour onto a parchment paper or lightly oiled sheet-pan to let cool.

Cinnamon Rolls (Sea-level Based Recipe):

1 cup Milk
¼ cup Butter
¼ cup Sugar
1 tsp Salt
1 Tbs dry yeast (1 pack)
¼ cup lukewarm Water
2 Eggs beaten
3 ½ cup All-Purpose, flour
4 Tbs melted butter

1 cup Sugar
1 tsp Cinnamon
1 cup Rasins
1 cup Chopped Nuts (your favorite)
    pecans are nice
1 cup powdered Sugar
1 Tbs Milk
½ tsp Vanilla

Method:
To make the dough:
Scald 1 cup of milk in pan and add ¼ cup butter, ¼ cup sugar and the salt. Set aside to cool. Dissolve the yeast in ¼ cup lukewarm water, until dissolved. Add milk and eggs. Gradually add the flour and mix until a soft dough is formed. Place on a floured table and knead until a smooth consistency, about 4-6 minutes. Punch it out and knead again for ½ minute. Allow dough to rest for 10 minutes.
To make the Rolls:
Roll out half of the dough into a rectangle to ¼ inch thickness. Brush with the melted butter. Combine the sugar, cinnamon, raisins and nuts. Spread half out on the dough. Roll up into a long log, and, with a sharp knife, cut into 1 inch pieces.
Place on a greased baking sheet. Repeat with other half of dough and filing. Cover and let rise for about 30-45 minutes or doubled in size. Bake in oven at 375°F for 15 – 25 minutes or until golden browned.

To make the gooey goodness coating: Combine the powdered sugar, 1 Tbs milk and vanilla… mix until smooth. Drizzle atop the warm rolls.

Country Style Peach Coffee Cake

6-8 Servings

1 cup peeled sliced Peaches
    (frozen peaches work too)
1 tsp Lemon juice
1 tsp Sugar
½ cup Butter, softened
1 Egg
1 tsp Vanilla
2 cups All-Purpose flour

1 ½ tsp Baking Powder
½ tsp Salt
½ cup Milk
1/3 cup All-Purpose flour
¼ cup Sugar
3 Tbs Butter, softened
¼ cup Pecans

Method of Preparation:

Combine the peaches, lemon juice, and 1 teaspoon sugar and set aside. Cream the butter, 1 cup of sugar and the egg until light in color. Add the vanilla. Sift 2 cups of flour, baking powder and salt. Add this to the creamed mixture also adding in the milk.

Pour into a greased and floured 9 inch square baking pan.

Drain the peaches and arrange on top of the batter.

TOPPING:

Combine the remaining flour and sugar and cut in the 3 Tablespoons of butter until mixture is crumbly. Add chopped nuts and sprinkle the mixture liberally over the peaches. Bake at 350°F for 1 hour.

NOTES:

EXTRAS and UPGRADES:

The extras section contains a couple of recipe enhancers and other tidbits and goodies. Look for future extras in the Kitchen Tech area of **www.JeepGrilleAdventures.com**

Make Ahead Chicken Stock and other Chicken Goodies for dual meals:

Make ahead and freeze in an ice tray or heavy duty Ziploc bag to thaw and use later for great flavor. It also won't contain nearly as much sodium as the canned stuff.
Makes ¾ Gallon

> 1 ea Whole Chicken, 2 ½ - 3 ½ lb.
> ¾ gallon Cold Water
> 1 ea *Bouquet Garni: Bay Leaf, ¼ cup Parsley Fresh, Peppercorns (wrap in cheesecloth or in a coffee filter)
> > *A fancy culinary term for an aromatic sack of flavor enhancements.
> 2 cups Carrots, Celery, Onion (mirepoix) and Garlic Cloves

Method of Preparation:

In a large pot, place the whole Chicken and the Bouquet Garni. Cover with cold water. Bring to a boil and reduce to simmer. Let simmer for 3 hours. During the last twenty minutes add the mirepoix. This allows for great flavor and full nutrient retention. If you add the mirepoix too early the flavor and nutrients of the vegetables cooks out.

Mirepoix: Fancy culinary term to impress your friends and relatives with. Use when referring to roughly chopped Carrots, Celery and Onions (could also include leeks if so desired).

Strain all the liquid and cool quickly. Pick all the meat from the chicken and chop or shred and COOL to under 40 degrees quickly.

This chicken meat is great with egg noodles and some fresh broth. Another great recipe is chicken pot pie or chicken with Cajun dirty rice and beans. The variety of items one can make from this simple procedure are endless!

IT'S NOT BURNT IT'S CAJUN STYLE!! Blackening Seasoning

2	cups Paprika		1/3	tsp Dry Thyme
½	cup Brown Sugar		1/3	tsp Dry Parsley
½	tsp Cayenne		1	Tbs Kosher Salt
1	tsp Granulated Garlic		½	Tbs cracked Black Pepper
½	tsp Coriander, ground			
¼	tsp Cumin, ground			

Method of Preparation:

Combine all the ingredients together.

Use to crust fish, beef, pork or chicken.

In a HOT (oil smoking) pan; sear the blacken crusted item on one side for 1 minute.

Turn and sear for another minute, finish cooking item in high temp oven.

Southwest Style Blackening Seasoning

I created this basic blend when I moved out west, it is a neat little spice rub that will start off sweet and turn into a slow heat.

2	cups	Chimayo or Light Chile Powder (medium or hot)	¼	tsp	Cumin
¼	cup	Brown Sugar	1/2	tsp	dry Cilantro Leaves
½	tsp	Cayenne	1	tsp	dry Parsley
1	tsp	Granulated Garlic	1	Tbs	Kosher Salt
½	tsp	Coriander	½	Tbs	cracked Black Pepper

Method of Preparation: Combine all the ingredients together. Use to crust fish, beef, pork or chicken. In a HOT (oil smoking) pan; sear the blacken crusted item on one side for 1 minute. Turn and sear for another minute, finish cooking item in high temp oven.

Moroccan Spice Blend:

This simple blend is awesome on American Lamb Kebabs or Lamb Rack.

2 tsp Crushed or Ground Coriander
1 tsp Ground Cumin
1 tsp Cinnamon, Ground
1 tsp Cardamom, Ground
1 tsp Paprika, Ground
½ tsp Turmeric, Ground

Method of Preparation: Lightly toast the above spices in a dry sauté pan.
Add Kosher Salt & Cracked Black Pepper to taste
This is one of my daughter's favorites, anything American Lamb, what a distinguished palate she has.

Chef D's Trinity Seasoning: For steaks and just about everything else I throw on the grille!

I use more of this than anything, of course it can be tweaked to suit your needs by adding herbs or other spices but I use a mix of equal pasts of Kosher Salt, Granulated Garlic and Fresh Ground Black Pepper. This is especially great rubbed on a whole prime rib, to slow roast. Of course adding your favorite dry herbs wouldn't hurt the mix either.

Basic Texas Style BBQ Rub: Thanks to my great chef friend, for this basic recipe, though he has since passed, and now commanding the grand kitchen in the sky. He was literally a walking culinary encyclopedia.
J.G. Boches - "Attention… CHEF ON DECK!!"
Use equal parts of fresh ground black pepper, paprika and granulated garlic. Add kosher salt to taste. Other things can be added to this to suit your personal tastes such as; ground mustard, cayenne pepper or chili powder. I have also added some pre-made Montreal Steak seasoning to this and it was wonderful.

Meat tricks: SLOW AND LOW just like crawlin' rocks in granny gear!!!!

Boneless Prime Rib: Season liberally, with The Trinity and some rosemary. Put the whole roast in roasting pan, place in preheated oven 450°F for 15 minutes. Drop the temperature down to 300°F. Let cook to an internal temperature of 120°F (use your culinary tire gauge) pull out of the oven to let rest, DO NOT CUT INTO IT, until rested for 10-15 minutes. Just trust me on this one. Slice and enjoy later on the trail as a roast beef sandwich.

Slow Roasted or Smoked Brisket: Season liberally with Basic Texas BBQ Rub. Place in roasting pan fat side up. Stab into the fat so as it cooks the fat drips down into the meat Put in preheated 195 - 200ºF oven. Close the oven door and "FUHGEDABOUTIT" for at least 20 hours. Can be covered with foil as well.

It should be finger tender (falls apart when you poke it). Put on some bread and BBQ sauce "M…MM….MMMM now that's some love in yo' mouth!"

Painted Desert Spice Blend

2 tsp Chimayo Chile Powder	1 tsp Brown Sugar
1 tsp Achiote Powdered or crumbled paste	1 tsp Paprika
	½ tsp Corriander, Ground
1 Tsp Chipotle Powder	1 Tbs Lime Juice
1 tsp Ground Cumin	1 Tbs Olive Oil
Kosher Salt & Cracked Black Pepper to taste	

This tends to be more of a wet rub style marinade. It will soak into and flavor the meat tremendously, giving it a vibrant color and awesome flavor.

Chef D Style Chimmi Churri (Argentinian Style Green Sauce)

Makes 1 Cup

This stuff goes well on ANYTHING grilled, meats, seafood or vegetable. It is so good I could drink it, no seriously.

½ Cup Olive Oil	1 Garlic Clove Peeled
¼ Cup Lime & Lemon Juice Mixture	1 tsp Red Onion
	1 Pinch Red Pepper Flakes
2 Tbsp Fresh Cilantro Leaves	Salt and Black Pepper - to taste
2 Tbsp Fresh Parsley Leaves	

Put all ingredients into a blender. Puree until smooth. Serve chilled. A different version can be chopping all of the ingredients very fine and mixing together for a more traditional style.

NOTES:

- 4-wheel responsibly! The saying here in Colorado is "Stay the trail!

- Camp responsibly! Be respectful of the outdoors and others in close proximity to your camp destination.

- Cook and eat safely and responsibly! Follow basic safe and sanitary food practices… nothing is worse than a case of food poisoning.

- *Drink RESPONSIBLY! I can't stress enough the importance of responsibly and safely consuming alcoholic beverages while in the backcountry or any country for that matter.

- PACK OUT WHAT YOU PACK IN!! I'll keep this one simple …"Your freekin' mothah doesn't live here!! So… pick your shit up and take it with you to dispose of properly. Leave no trace! Capisca, Begrijp, Comprenez, καταλάβετε, Compreenda, поймите, entienda, UNDERSTAND!?!?"

By practicing the above, groups like the Sierra Club, have less ammunition to fuel their fight. It is because of ignorant jackasses, wheeling off the legal road/trail/route, driving drunk, leaving trash and/or breaking glass bottles scattered throughout public lands that ruin it for the rest of us, and, the potential future access to these beautiful areas. Back in the late 1970's and early 1980's I witnessed the massive closure of large areas of the Cape Cod National Seashore, the fond outdoor memories of my youth. I don't want to witness anything like that again, nor do I want my children to witness similar actions.

I say this candidly and with the utmost Massachusetts demeanor in respect to being a responsible individual utilizing the outdoors:
"Don't be a freekin' tahd!"

Support your rights and access to public lands.
Realize this applies to more than just the 4x4 folks, some extreme
groups want complete closure of public lands to all; recreational
motor-sport, bicyclists, horseback and foot hiking.
Yes, they want all access closed to you and me!!!

"Live Free or Die!" N.H. State Motto.

Written by General John Stark, July 31, 1809. The motto became "Live Free Or Die," as once voiced by General John Stark, the New Hampshire's most distinguished hero of the Revolutionary War, and the world famous Old Man of the Mountain was voted the official state emblem.

The motto was part of a volunteer toast which General Stark sent to his wartime comrades, in which he declined an invitation to head up a 32nd anniversary reunion of the 1777 Battle of Bennington in Vermont, because of poor health. The toast said in full: "Live Free Or Die; Death Is Not The Worst of Evils." The following year, a similar invitation (also declined) said: "The toast, sir, which you sent us in 1809 will continue to vibrate with unceasing pleasure in our ears, "Live Free Or Die; Death Is Not The Worst Of Evils. http://www.nh.gov/nhinfo/emblem.html 7/29/07

For the 4x4 and Off Highway Recreational Vehicle Crowd:
Blue Ribbon Coalition
http://www.sharetrails.org/

Tread Lightly
http://www.treadlightly.org/

THIS IS THE END….THE ONLY END MY FRIEND:

So the trip ends as so often they do… the conclusion if you will…concluding what?!
An end but to what?!
An experience of body, mind, and soul that is a glimpse in time to once again yearn and aspire to yet another day.
Creating a mental picture for others to venture forth, yielding unto the continuum, rather than a conclusion.
I leave you with the desire and aspiration of adventure… take only one and you're addicted.
Yearning and aspiring, to see what lies ahead.
Life on this endless journey has taken me here, in the blink of and eye it has passed and taken me there.
Where….? To the beginning rather than the end….

EAT WELL, WHEEL WELL and RESPONSIBLY…..SEE YOU ON THE TRAIL CALLED ADVENTURE!

Thank you,
Mark M. DeNittis a/k/a Chef D

CONTACTS & FRIENDS in the making of JEEP GRILLE ADVENTURE: Where to get the good stuff!

Crawletech 4x4/Crane Hi-Clearance
4785 Elati St #33 Denver Co 80216
720-422-4598
www.crawlertech4x4.com

Homestyle Bakery, Grand Junction, CO
(970) 243-1233
924 N 7th St Grand Junction, CO 81501-3108

Carmine Lonardo's Italian Meat
Market/Deli
(303) 699-4532 15380 E Smoky Hill Rd
        Aurora, CO 80015-1492
(303) 985-3555 7585 W Florida Ave
        Lakewood, CO 80232-5407

Colorado's Best Beef, Boulder, CO
http://www.cobestbeef.com/
303-449-8632 or 1-866-414-BEEF (2333)

Coffea Rostir, Denver, CO
www.coffearostir.com
303-283-4077
10890 E. Dartmouth Ave.
Denver CO 80014

Villa Tatra Smokehouse, Pinewood CO   Ww
303-823-6819
729 Pinewood Dr. Lyons CO 80540
www.villatatra.com

Oskar Blues Brewery, Lyons CO
303 823-6685
303 Main St. Lyons CO 80540
www.oskarblues.com

www.JPFreek.com Adventure Magazine
The Official Digital Publication of Jeep
Jamboree USA
www.7BarGrille.com & Culinary
Modification Tools, Get some…spice in yo'
life!

RMHE Enterprise, Denver CO
www.rmhenterprises.com
4785 Elati #32 80216 Denver, CO
303-808-1268

Avalanche Engineering, Durango, CO
http://www.avalancheengineering.com/
40039 Hwy 160 Bayfield, CO 81122 Phone:
970.884.7716

Advance Adapters Inc. California
http://www.advanceadapters.com/

www.4x4Wire.com
All over the place

John Folse and Company
http://www.jfolse.com/

Red Rock 4 Wheelers;
THE MECCA Moab, UT
http://www.rr4w.com/

DUOR Club: Denver University
Offroad Club and Friends
http://www.du.edu/orgs/DUOR

High Country Performance 4x4
1695 West Hamilton
Place Englewood CO 80110
Ph: (303) 761-7379 Fax: (303) 761-4950
www.HCP4x4.com

Get your dose of Adventure Travel and Fine Dining from:
www.JPFreek.com and www.7BarGrille.com

CULINARY MODIFICATION TOOLS

Each C.M.T. tin contains 4 – 6 ounces (dependant on density of individual ingredients) of the highest quality spice blends. Each tin on average, dependant on user tastes and recipe inclusion can easily produce multiple servings. The beverage C.M.T.'s will make approximately 1 – 1 ½ gallon of pure liquid refreshment pleasure.

WARNING..... FOOD MODIFICATIONS MAY CAUSE EXTREME ADDICTION!

HELL'S REVENGE TRAIL DUST: A dry version of the very well known Buffalo style hot sauce without the liquidy mess! Classic hot sauce flavor with buttery notes, use on grilled or fried chicken, pork, fish or any version of potato, this seasoning will likely spice up the best of foods.

LAS CRUCES CHILE CHALLENGE: Warming the southwestern soul and spirit this seasoning will enhance any chicken or pork green chile dish that you and your guests will come to love. Pork or Chicken Green Chile goes great as any breakfast egg dish topping or stand alone with soft flour tortillas. Works great mixed with sour cream as a chip dip, steak or chop seasoning, as well sprinkled on potatoes! If you're really hardcore like the trails around Las Cruces you'll probably spoon it straight down!

SOUTHERN SLAM B.B.Q. RUB: Description: Put some south in yo' mouth with this classic B.B.Q. seasoning. Rub liberally on pork ribs, chicken legs or breasts or beef brisket or meaty back ribs and add some smoke…and not the smoke from your tailpipe.

STUCK IN THE MUD SPUD SPICE: Classic hash brown potato taste this can also be used to spice up mashed potatoes, baked potatoes, French fries or homemade potato chips.

SWAMP STOMPIN' BAYOU SPICE: Enjoy the "down-home" flavors of the deep-south's bayou country with this Cajun style seasoning. Use sparingly or heartily to enhance your next Cajun style chicken, pork or fish dish. Remember, it's not burnt…it's blackened!

DIE TRYING STEAK RUB: Just like the Moab trail you'll crave the adrenaline rush of mouth watering flavors with this steak seasoning. Hints of balsamic and herb flavors make this a steak seasoning an unparalleled crowd pleaser. Heck you can even make tofu taste good with this stuff.

RUBICON'S ULTIMATE BURGER BANG: This burger modification tool will surely conquer the most challenging of crowds appetites. From traversing the mighty Rubicon itself or your backyard patio the Ultimate Rubicon Burger Bang will enhance your cooking prowess.

WE'VE GOT YOUR ADVENTURE THIRSTS COVERED TOO!

POISON SPIDER BLOODY MARY MIX: Use this dual purpose seasoning when making a virgin or fully loaded Bloody Mary or mix with ground meat for an outstanding meatloaf.

BIG HORN MOUNTAIN MAN COCOA: With a hint of Ancho chile this hot cocoa will be a hit.

KILLINGTON'S "KILLAH" CIDER: Warming thoughts of this classic hot cider mulling spice for those cold nights.

4x4Wire

http://www.4x4wire.com/outdoor/trailbites/jerky.htm
http://www.4x4wire.com/outdoor/trailbites/driedfruit/
http://www.4x4wire.com/outdoor/trailbites/nuts/
http://www.4x4wire.com/trail/report/ca/tds01a/
http://www.4x4wire.com/trail/report/ca/tds01b/
http://www.4x4wire.com/outdoor/trailbites/stoves/
http://www.4x4wire.com/feature/chefmark/summer03/
http://www.4x4wire.com/outdoor/trailbites/seafood/
http://www.4x4wire.com/trail/cooking/recipes/
http://www.4x4wire.com/feature/chefmark/summer05/
http://www.4x4wire.com/outdoor/trailbites/hunt_camp/

COLORADO FOREST SERVICE CONTACTS
http://www.fs.fed.us/r2/recreation/map/colorado/

Business Hours
Monday-Friday
7:30 a.m.–4:30 p.m. MT

Phone
303-275-5350
303-275-5367 for the hearing impaired

Other Disclaimers:
1. Small portions of this book contain a mild version of "Massachusetts" or "Back-East" style of expression or attitude fondly known as humor to those of us from there. Most, not from anywhere near there, might consider or deem it offensive or hurtful to their 'um…feelings. If you are offended I could offer several antidotes for your problem, the best and most useful of course would be…."Put it in 4-lo and get over it"!!!

2. MUCH MORE IMPORTANTLY: Although you would think most people would be responsible and accept responsibility for their own actions I am including this to cover my ass.*RMTE, LLC and its representatives neither implies nor indicates and certainly does not condone driving or operating any mechanical equipment while under the influence of alcohol, when using recipes including Optional Adult Friendly alcohol ingredients. RMTE, LLC and its representatives does not take responsibility for your personal actions or the personal actions of others nor will be held liable for your personal actions or the personal actions of others when/while utilizing and/or consuming alcohol related ingredients within the JGA Camp Kitchen & Cookbook series. Remember: "Don't be a freekin tahd!"

3. On a much lighter note, although very serious to some: No animals were intentionally hurt during the production of this book. Some various bugs may have inadvertently been smashed against the windshield or been consumed by the grille of the Jeep (damn Jeeps get hungry too!). Some small ground critters, bugs or slightly larger critters, may have accidentally succumb to the rolling of 31, 32, 33 or 35 inch rubber meats of my Jeep's tire history. This by no means was intentional…at all, especially any de-clawing of live lobsters. Finally as far as I know, all animal proteins, plants or otherwise consumed to this point to produce this book, or otherwise, have been treated fairly and in a humane manner, if not… really "What'll mean in a hundred years?" Blues Traveler. If you feel otherwise, again I suggest "Put it in 4-Lo and get over it!!! No…really… get a life!"

Don't forget to checkout….
http://www.cafepress.com/adventureware
…for the latest and greatest JGA Bling!

ABOUT THE AUTHOR:

Born in Worcester, MA and spending the better part of twenty-one years there, growing up in full size vehicles I always had a "whikked" (it's a Mass thing and folks from there would understand) passion for the outdoors.

I have since traveled throughout New England and in 1993 with my life packed in an '88 Bronco headed south and didn't look back. Wild and wonderful West Virginia, West Palm Beach, Florida, then westward "GO WEST YOUNG MAN" ending up near Granby, Colorado. I traded in the Bronco for the first rollout of the Jeep TJ with round headlights, you know a real authentic Jeep with round headlights and all…ha-ha, just kidding had to mess with all the YJ and Cherokee Folks on that one (it's a Jeep thing). Of course this was much smaller than what I was used to driving and wheeling but… YEEE HAW!

Since graduating in 1992 with an Associates Degree in culinary arts from Johnson & Wales University in Providence, R.I., I have had a successful career in my chosen field of study. While attending JWU I was fortunate enough to obtain a three month externship at the Breakers Hotel Resort of Palm Beach, Florida, which I would later go back to work for an additional two years. "The foundations of excellence and industry work ethic were instilled at The Breakers".

Cumulative years of experience have developed a well-rounded perspective, with expertise in the food and beverage industry on several levels. Having numerous years of experience both in industry and now several years in adult education at one of the premier Culinary Institutions in the country, Johnson & Wales University, has allowed me to further cultivate my professional career.

My writing style has come a long way since my first story book at age 4, ten pages of colored 2x2 note pad paper titled, The Snake, my father Matt is quoted as saying "I always knew you would do something with writing in life", thanks Dad, while Mom, probably still has the original copy somewhere amongst all of my other things she has saved of mine.

Most recently I have joined the team at www.JPFreek.com Adventure Magazine and Official Digital Publication of Jeep Jamboree USA. Other well known accolades include being a published food editor for www.4x4Wire.com, an online magazine with my Trail Bites series. Having also at age 23 been featured as one of the Ranch Chefs in The Great Ranch Cookbook 1996, by Gwen Ashley Walters, my literary style has since developed and filtered into many aspects of the foodservice educational sector. In addition to teaching I have been an educational consultant to the American Lamb Board having authored several articles, training materials and DVD script, inclusive of being the on camera spokesperson.

"I continue to strive for excellence and further develop myself with as much passion and vigor as I had when I was a B.A.M.F'n line cook (those who know, know what a B.A.M.F'n line cook is). "It's an old school chef thing…you wouldn't understand"!

"Realize, cooking isn't rocket science, have fun! Recipes are guidelines, use them as a base and create your own flair and fond food and family memories (say that 10 times fast). I've spent the first thirty years of life working hard…it's time to spend the rest of it working smart! "Now make like a tree… get outta heayah… and go hit the frickin whicked trails man, all with killah grub from My Jeep Grille Adventures, hope to see you out there!"

Mark M. DeNittis "Chef D"

Made in the USA